# THE CREATIVE PROFESSIONAL'S
# GUIDE TO
# MONEY

### How to think about it. How to talk about it.
### How to manage it.

**Ilise Benun**
**founder of** Marketing-Mentor.com

**BOOKS**
Cincinnati, Ohio
www.howdesign.com

For more excellent books and resources for designers, visit www.howdesign.com.

15  14  13  12  11      5 4 3 2 1

Distributed in Canada by Fraser Direct, 100 Armstrong Avenue, Georgetown, Ontario, Canada L7G 5S4, Tel: (905) 877-4411. Distributed in the U.K and Europe by F+W Media International, Brunel House, Newton Abbot, Devon, TQ12 4PU, England, Tel: (+44) 1626-323200, Fax: (+44) 1626-323319, E-mail: postmaster@davidandcharles.co.uk. Distributed in Australia by Capricorn Link, P.O. Box 704, Windsor, NSW 2756 Australia, Tel: (02) 4577-3555.

Library of Congress Cataloging-in-Publication Data

Benun, Ilise, 1961-
   The creative professional's guide to money / Ilise Benun.
      p. cm.
   Includes index.
   ISBN 978-1-4403-0243-5 (pbk. : alk. paper)
   1. Artists--Finance, Personal. 2. Self-employed--Finance, Personal. 3. Small business--Finance. I. Title.
   HG179.B423 2011
   332.024--dc22

                        2010045261

Edited by Amy Schell Owen
Designed by Grace Ring
Cover photography ©iStockphoto.com/DLeonis
Production coordinated by Greg Nock

## ABOUT THE AUTHOR

Ilise Benun is an author, consultant and national speaker, founder of Marketing-Mentor.com, and co-producer of the Creative Freelancer Conference.

Her books include *The Designer's Guide to Marketing and Pricing* (HOW Books), *Stop Pushing Me Around: A Workplace Guide for the Timid, Shy and Less Assertive* (Career Press), *Self-Promotion Online* (HOW Books), *Designing Web Sites:// for Every Audience* (HOW Books) and *The Art of Self Promotion.* She also co-authored *Public Relations for Dummies, 2nd Edition* (John Wiley & Sons) with Eric Yaverbaum and Bob Bly.

Her work has been featured in national publications such as *HOW* magazine, *Inc., Self, Essence, Crain's New York Business, Dynamic Graphics, Working Woman, The New York Times, The Globe and Mail, The Washington Post, The Denver Post* and more.

Benun has given presentations for international organizations, including the American Marketing Association, Business Marketing Association, National Association of Women Business Owners, HOW Design Conference, Freelancers Union, AIGA, Graphic Artists Guild, Registered Graphic Designers of Ontario, Advertising Photographers of America, American Society of Media Photographers, Editorial Freelancers Association, New York Public Library, NYU Entrepreneurship Summit, 92nd St. Y and many ad clubs around the country.

From her home office in Hoboken, New Jersey, Benun spends her days coaching creative professionals who are serious about growing their business, one-on-one and in small groups. She started her business in 1988 and has been self-employed for all but three years of her working life. She has a B.A. in Spanish from Tufts University. For more infomation, please visit: www.marketing-mentor.com.

## ACKNOWLEDGMENTS

Writing is thought to be a solitary activity, one person alone with a blank piece of paper (or a blank screen these days, although I still like paper). But that's not how this book was written.This book represents my most collaborative effort to date. I sought out as many people as would agree to participate, and they were, in the end, numerous: from clients who shared their experiences and stories with me to subject matter experts, whose ideas I absorbed as we talked. They all shared perspectives that complemented, strengthened and sometimes also conflicted with my own.

I can't list everyone here but I will try. It all started with a conversation between me and Peleg Top, my co-author of *The Designer's Guide to Marketing and Pricing*. Our friend Tom Tombusch of Wordstream Copy drafted the first proposal. Amy Owen and Megan Patrick at HOW Books helped us shape it, accepted it and then trusted me to deliver when it started to morph into something else entirely. Thank you both for your trust.

During the research phase I talked to colleagues and industry professionals who took the time to share their experiences, including Susan Chait, Emily Cohen, Monique Elwell, Cameron Foote, Galia Gichon, Rick Gould, Kit Hinrichs, Lee Jacobson, Maya Kopytman, JP Lacroix, Dana Manciagli, Frank Marciano, Jennifer Neal, Mona Patel, Shel Perkins, Jean Perwin, Jennifer Rittner, Lee Silber, Michael Steger, Andy Strote, Mikelann Valterra, Petrula Vrontikis, June Walker and Jon Weiman.

Near the end of the writing phase, my ad hoc editorial team read pages of unfinished thoughts and sent me their comments and, in one case, went over them with me, line by line. Those generous people were Jonathan Cleveland, Doug Dolan, Nina Felshin, Galia Gichon, Aaron Joslow, Dana Manciagli, Patrice Robertie, Rhonda Schaller, Alan Seiden.

There were a few who went further: Dyana Valentine, the worksheet queen, got out of her sickbed one Saturday morning to brainstorm better worksheets. Besides everything he'd already done, Doug Dolan was on call near the end of this process to stop everything he was doing to give me feedback on a new idea for the introduction. And James Tricarico gets a month of homemade dinners in exchange for hours spent explaining accounting basics to me.

I have come to depend on the F+W Media gang as we work on more projects together and their effect on my business deepens. In fact, I realize that if it weren't for this almost twenty-year association with F+W, a lot of the people I cite above wouldn't have found their way to me in the first place. So a big thanks for any peripheral (and future) support that has seeped into this book project goes to Bryn Mooth, Beth Dean, SueAnn Stein, Larry Zimmer, Cory Smith, Gary Lynch and Kate Rados.

Also at F+W Media and mostly behind the scenes has been book designer, Grace Ring, who I trust to take my words and make them easy to read. And, of course my editor, Amy Owen, who has shepherded this project through with patience and encouragement.

I certainly wouldn't be where I am today without my support system behind the scenes: copywriter extraordinaire, Deidre Rienzo (you're the best!), Kathleen Harrington and David Tornabene, Cathy Baehler, Pamela Strell, The Haas Family, Maria McKenna, Luz Ossa, Dr. S and all of my sisters.

It's new for me to be grateful to so many people for so much, but I am truly awed and humbled by the generosity of everyone who contributed to this book, whether you knew it or not.

I thank you all.

## ABOUT MARKETING MENTOR

Marketing-Mentor.com is a resource for creative professionals who are serious about growing their creative business. We help you focus on pricing, marketing, time management and general business development, plus how it all fits into the rest of your life.

Working with beginners and veteran creative professionals, solopreneurs and small firm owners, we offer one-on-one coaching, group coaching and workshops to teach you how to structure the business that meets your needs, how to get the clients you want and, hopefully, how to have more control over your life.

We help you set realistic goals, show you how to reach them and then keep you on track until you do. We act as a sophisticated sounding board while also providing resources, then we point you in the right direction so you can do what needs to be done. With Marketing Mentor by your side, you'll learn how to make your creative business work for you.

In our online store, Marketing-Mentor-Toolbox.com, you will also find tools and information products you can use to stay on track and take your business to the next level, including the Start Anytime Marketing Plan + Calendar and its electronic counterpart, the Marketing eCalendar.

Visit www.marketing-mentor.com to take advantage of the free half-hour phone mentoring session—don't worry, it's not a sales pitch. It's just a way to get a taste of how Marketing Mentor can help grow your business.

### MARKETING MENTOR
1012 Park Ave, Hoboken, NJ 07030
phone: (201) 653-0783
e-mail: ilise@marketing-mentor.com
website: www.marketing-mentor.com

# CONTENTS

# FOREWORD

When my father used to advise us kids on making the right career choices, he'd inevitably say, "Do what you love and the money will look after itself."

Of course, this was the same man whose counsel on the temptations of teenage sex was summed up in the warning, "Five seconds of pleasure aren't worth a lifetime of misery." Even at thirteen, I could see that the absurdity of those words was matched only by their poignancy. But on the whole money-looking-after-itself thing, the old man was—well, right on the money. In fact, I've offered the same advice to my own kids, with absolute conviction.

The only problem is it's not true.

Money is far too important to be left alone in the hope that it will somehow look after itself, like a leaky tap or a marriage that's started to drift. Come to think of it, those don't really take care of themselves, either. But we're talking about money here. And money definitely takes work.

The challenge, if you're going to offer advice in this area, is coming up with something that hasn't been said before by—I don't know—Adam Smith. John Maynard Keynes. Pink Floyd. That weird little guy with the pancake makeup in *Cabaret*.

Well, my friend Ilise Benun has shown that there is quite a bit more to say on the subject. This book is aimed at creative types, but it's equally valuable to anyone who has a special talent to offer the world but hasn't quite figured out how to get people to pay for it. Ilise has woven together helpful tips and cautionary tales from her own consulting practice and a whole network of creative practitioners who (if I'm at all representative) have made their share of stupid money moves and now feel compelled to warn the others. The result is a wealth of guidance on deciding how much you're worth, presenting that figure with a straight face and then managing all the nuances of what happens next if, to your astonishment, someone actually agrees to your price.

As Ilise has worked on this project, she's kindly invited me to chime in now and then with war stories and odd realizations that have struck me as I blunder through the business world seeking payment for my services. Now she's flattered me all the more by asking if I'll step in front of the curtain to offer a few opening remarks. And I'm not even being paid—which I suppose doesn't speak well of my own negotiating skills.

Anyway, because Ilise has graciously asked me to go first, I'll corroborate what she covers in far richer detail by throwing out three key things I've learned about the financial side of being a creative professional:

**1. Everyone is uncomfortable talking about money.** If you feel awkward bringing it up, rest assured that your client feels equally uneasy. That's why it typically takes so long to steer conversations around to the bottom line. People are no more comfortable talking about money than they are discussing their sex lives—sadly, maybe even less so.

Knowing this doesn't necessarily make it easier to justify your fee or navigate through whatever negotiations are needed to land a piece of business. But it should at least dispel the illusion that the person on the other side of the desk is supremely confident on the whole money question and is just sitting there, fingers drumming on the trap-door lever, waiting for you to say something stupid.

**2. Never apologize for a price.** That's basically saying that you can't defend it. And if you can't defend the fee for your services, you'd better head back to the calculator and figure out what you *can* justify—which is a pretty awkward thing to do in the middle of a meeting. So get it right the first time. Then declare it firmly, try not to blink and, who knows, prospective clients may actually say yes.

And if, on the other hand, they tell you they can get the same thing elsewhere for less, admit it readily: "Sure, you'll always be able to find someone who can beat me on price alone. But as you know," —even though they may not— "it's a question of comparing apples to apples on issues like quality, experience and service." Of course, they may in fact have found better apples than yours—in which case, that's show biz. But at least you haven't immediately crumbled and offered to lower your fee, which is a sure way to lose respect and won't guarantee you the job anyway. Often they just want to see if you'll do it.

**3. Always know the absolute lowest price you'll settle for.** Figure out that number ahead of time—test it every which way to make sure you're happy with how you got there—and then stick to it, no matter what. Otherwise you'll hate yourself later. Also, just because you've got your minimum safety net in place, don't jump into it at the first sign of a wobble in the negotiations. Show some serious, brow-knitting hesitation in moving down to the price you've secretly told yourself you could live with. Because if you get sucked into trying to seem like the earnest, obliging supplier of their dreams, again you'll end up regretting it. Five seconds of pleasure aren't worth a lifetime of misery.

So that's my two cents' worth to introduce Ilise's far more valuable offering. This is the book I badly needed twenty-odd years ago. Who am I kidding? I still need it today. If you take only a fraction of the advice in these pages, you can count on a solid return on your investment. You probably won't even feel awkward talking about it. And that's money in the bank.

**—DOUG DOLAN**

(www.dougdolan.com)

# INTRODUCTION

Are you weird about money?

By weird, I mean does it make you behave strangely? Make you say and do things that are uncharacteristic of who you are (or who you think you are or who you want to be)? Do you wish "the money thing" would just get taken care of so you didn't have to deal with it?

When I'm "weird" about any aspect of my life, things tend to get overly complicated. Fuzzy gray areas make for mucho anxiety. Sometimes even chaos.

It doesn't have to be that way. I know because I've had to face my own weirdness about money, among other things. I started my business in 1988, when I was essentially forced into self-employment after being fired from my second job out of college, and I knew nothing! Nothing about business, about communication, about marketing, about money. I disguised my ignorance with what my grandmother called "chutzpah," but chutzpah doesn't go very deep and it can't take you very far. Eventually I needed to build a substantial foundation for my business, if it was going to support me.

That meant I had to learn a few things. Of course, the richest lessons came from my worst mistakes, and thinking back, the source of almost every problem was miscommunication. I was too often too afraid to ask for clarification when I didn't understand. Or I left things vague when I wasn't sure what I was doing, which inevitably caused problems, especially in the realm of money.

Fast forward twenty-three years and I have indeed learned a thing or two. I've gotten better at weeding out clients who don't pay, because with experience, I've learned to spot them a mile away. By fumbling for words or saying the wrong thing, I've learned how to say clearly what I charge, then shut up so the other person can respond. It isn't always a positive response but I don't expect them all to be. I only need enough positive responses to make my monthly income goal.

The most valuable lesson for me has been to approach every aspect of my work every single day as one grand experiment. The outcome I'm most interested in is learning, so the attitude I strive for is, "This negotiation (or proposal or huge presentation or whatever!) is an exercise." That means that every new project or client represents not only a new job but also a new opportunity to get better at doing business. Every negotiation is not a chance at more money but the chance to become a better communicator. If I succeed at that, the money does in fact take care of itself, as Doug's dad predicted (see Foreword).

As a creative professional, it's unlikely you've had any training in business or money. That would explain not being an expert in dealing with it—and it isn't genetic. So you too will make mistakes (and probably have). You will spend more time than you should on a project and you will lose money. This is how you will learn. And it is through this learning process that you will get better at all of it and begin to feel more confident. In fact, your mistakes will teach you more than this book, but you can use this book to make fewer—and less serious—mistakes. I've tried to offer some tools and techniques that have worked for me and my clients, right down to actual examples of language you can adapt to your own style and situations.

Money should be matter-of-fact, dealt with like any other aspect of a project. You address the issues as they arise, then discuss and resolve any differences, without emotion, without fantasy and without any unnecessary complicating factors. Not too weird, is it?

Read on...

# PART ONE

# HOW TO
# THINK ABOUT IT

# SELF ASSESSMENT:
# HOW DO YOU THINK ABOUT MONEY?

· · · · · · · · · · · · · · · · · · · · · · · · · · · · · · · · · · · · · · · · · · · · · · · · ·

- ☐ I don't like dealing with money.
- ☐ I'm not a "business person."
- ☐ I don't have self-confidence.
- ☐ I don't like putting a price on my work.
- ☐ I obsess over "the money thing" and complicate it, when I sense it could be simple.
- ☐ I haven't been trained so I feel ignorant about money.
- ☐ I lower my prices even if the client doesn't ask me to.

· · · · · · · · · · · · · · · · · · · · · · · · · · · · · · · · · · · · · · · · · · · · · · · · ·

Where does money figure into your life as a creative professional? How good are you at handling it? How comfortable are you talking about it? How well have you planned around it?

If you're like many creative professionals, especially if you checked any of the boxes above, chances are you haven't quite mastered the money thing. Whether quoting prices to a client, charging enough for your services or paying attention to your bottom line, you could be doing better.

So what follows are some tools for helping you do better. Let's get started.

# CHAPTER 1
# THE BUSINESS MIND-SET

"You get what you demand, not necessarily what you deserve."

**—MIKELANN VALTERRA, CERTIFIED FINANCIAL RECOVERY COACH AND AUTHOR**

Can you make a successful living doing what you love?

Yes, you can—but only if you decide to take it seriously and treat it like a business.

Let's start by looking back. When you started your career, was money even in the equation and how so? Was it love of the craft and creative expression that drove you? Did you assume money would take care of itself or you would figure it out eventually?

Most people who go into business do so because they want, first and foremost, to be a business owner. That's not usually the case with creative professionals. You see yourself as a creative first, and you love the creative work. You're in business, whether as a freelancer or running a larger entity, by accident rather than by design. You may have jumped or perhaps were pushed. If you're lucky, with a combination of talent and excellent timing, you have ridden a wave of "success." If you aren't so lucky, it's been a struggle, but you're still here. Either way, there are aspects of the business that are not your favorite, and dealing with money is probably one of them.

Self-employment offers an opportunity to take control of so many aspects of your life, to become less dependent on one entity to provide everything for you. Being your own boss— whether you choose to be a solopreneur or run a firm of any size—allows you to take on that responsibility, in essence that freedom.

And yet, so few self-employed people are actually in control of their business. This does not come naturally to many creative professionals, nor is it taught in art school. And there is a lot to learn—especially about money—if you want to have a profitable and healthy enterprise with high-quality clients, interesting projects and a strong foundation that doesn't collapse the moment the economy shifts.

This book will help, but only if you're serious about getting a handle on your finances.

## SEE YOURSELF AS A BUSINESS

Many creative professionals hang out their shingles or open their doors for business, then proceed to wait and hope: hoping clients will find them, hoping they'll get enough work, hoping the client will pay the bill, hoping the checks add up at the end of the month so all the bills get paid. If you think about it, it's a very passive position, taking what comes along instead of deciding what you want and pursuing it.

There is an alternative, and it is within your reach. You can replace the passive mind-set with planning and action. The first step is to re-envision yourself as a business. But what exactly does that mean?

At the core, it's a shift in the way you see yourself, a small shift that can affect every little detail about how you do your work and especially how far you go.

## Understand the Difference Between Spending and Investing

Whether you realize it or not, your personal perspective on money affects your decision-making process in business and, therefore, your ultimate success. In fact, if you have had no training in finances or business, it can be the difference between a prosperous and a struggling business.

One essential concept to understand is the difference between spending and investing. When you, as an individual, buy something, you are spending money. The more you spend, the less you have. Even if you spend your personal money as an investment—in your comfort, your happiness or your children's education—the goal isn't a tangible "return" on that investment, as it is in business.

When a business spends money—this includes your business—there is an expected return. When purchases are made with the express intention of making more money, the price paid is not as important as the return on the investment (ROI). Ideally, the greater the investment, the greater the potential return on investment.

This difference between spending and investing is also important when you make financial decisions for your business. Whatever your business decides to purchase should have a benefit (return) that outweighs its cost. For example, upgrades in computers or software should pay back more than their cost by enabling faster workflow, or by allowing you to attract enough new clients to more than pay for itself. Or, if you decide to invest between $5,000 and $10,000 to exhibit at a trade show, you should be able to project the potential return on that investment before deciding whether to do it.

Remembering the difference between spending and investing will also help when it comes to pricing your services. Your prices, whether high or low, are for services designed to help your clients achieve their goals, to get a return on their investment—by expanding their organization, enhancing their brand or increasing their sales. That means your price may not be the deal-breaker you imagine. Often it is only one of many factors in their decision-making process. You must be able to confidently make the argument that a greater investment (i.e. a higher price) can provide a greater return. When you have adopted a business mind-set, you will.

## Be Objective About Your Work

Taking your business seriously also means being as objective as possible. But as a creative, your work is more than a "job." You are probably emotionally attached to the work you do. You may even pour your heart and soul into it.

This can present a problem. According to Jon Weiman, designer and adjunct professor at Pratt Institute, "Creative professionals have trouble because they tie their ego and self-worth to the work in a way that is not businesslike. It becomes too personal."

### Know There Is No Absolute Value to Your Work

Many creatives complain about working with clients who don't value their work. But the problem isn't the clients or the work. You can't force a client to value your work the way you do. You can only seek, and hopefully find, the clients who do value what you do. But that requires time and effort. They don't always come knocking unbidden on your door.

There is much hand wringing around the idea of getting "what you're worth" or "what you deserve." In fact, there is nothing objective about it. Value itself is both subjective and subject to change. What has value to you may have less or more to a client. And what has value to one client today may have more or less tomorrow because of any number of factors, including a shift in their priorities, in the economy and in what they perceive to be their options—most of this you don't control or even know about.

With a business mind-set, you are aware of this subjectivity and fluidity. You learn about your prospect or client, you come to an agreement on price and you do your best work. When you make a mistake, you learn from it for next time.

### Get Out of the Financial Fog

What? You're not a "numbers person"? Your head goes fuzzy when someone starts talking numbers? All the intelligence you exhibit in other areas of your life seems to evaporate? Somehow you can no longer do the multiplication you learned at age nine?

One of the reasons this aspect of your business may be confusing is because you have not been trained in the financial aspects of business like a business school graduate has. Which isn't to say you need a business degree to run a business. But you do need training and guidance from professionals.

Creatives often say, "I'm not good with money," which more than anything is a self-fulfilling prophecy, primarily of a psychological nature, and it's important to deal with. Suffice it to say, you're not alone. There is hope, as this fuzziness is not a genetic condition.

Also, there are few common financial definitions. In fact, the accounting field is filled with terms that all mean the same thing, and no organization has been successful in coming up with a standard glossary. Don't get hung up on terminology and don't throw up your hands in confusion. Instead, get educated and get help.

In reality, money is simple and logical. It doesn't conflict with or corrupt your creativity. It's math, after all, and most of it is not all that complicated. Numbers either add up or they don't. If they don't, there's something wrong, and if you look closely, you can usually figure out what it is. But not if you've already decided you can't or just don't get it. That's up to you. It just takes attention—focused attention.

"There is a lot of shame that surrounds issues of money," says Mikelann Valterra, director of the Women's Earning Institute. "It is as if we say to ourselves, 'What is wrong with me that I can't figure this out?' It is frustrating, because we know we are intelligent. But why then do we fall into self-defeating patterns around money? The truth is that money issues go far beyond our intellect. Money taps into our deepest emotions and symbolizes what we fear, hope for and desire in life."

Listen to an interview with Mikelann Valterra at www.creative freelancerblog.com /money-guide.

## Be Confident About Money

Your prospects and clients need you to be confident. They are looking for confidence in their vendors and resources. They want to be persuaded that they will be in good hands if they choose you.

But many creative professionals experience a lack of confidence, which usually has nothing to do with the quality of the work. Instead it seems to stem from comparisons you make between you and your competitors, who are sometimes also your friends and colleagues, which makes it tricky. You may feel "less than" if you are self-taught at your profession and they have a degree or some other credential that is perceived as valuable. Or perhaps you don't feel comfortable calling yourself an "expert" or, worse, you imagine yourself as an imposter and therefore can't charge prices level with someone with more credentials. All of this may prevent you from reassuring your prospects and securing the projects you want.

Self-confidence is an element of taking your business seriously. It requires that you shift your attention away from what you imagine others think and refocus your attention on real-time actions—yours and theirs. It takes time, practice and experience to develop this confidence, so be patient with yourself. And as it develops, you might need to fake it a bit, speaking and acting as if you already possess it. That's okay because confidence sometimes begets confidence. And it builds when you earn at your potential. Valterra says, "There is nothing that compares to the feeling of self-confidence and self-reliance that making money provides us."

> ## PRACTICE MAKES CONFIDENT
> ## WHEN IT COMES TO TALKING ABOUT MONEY
>
> One way to break the cycle of avoiding the "money conversation" is to do exactly the opposite: make a habit of talking money from the very beginning of a project and keep bringing it up all the way through.
>
> Dana Manciagli, general manager of a large division of Microsoft, suggests making it a part of your process to talk money during the last five minutes of every conversation. "I want a proactive business partner, not just a creative. I would love it if a creative said, 'I understand you're accountable for every dime you spend, so every Friday I will call or send you a message about where you stand on your budget.' Like a weekly budget check-in. That way, there are no surprises."

## THE TROUBLE WITH MONEY

So what's the problem with money? Granted, it's a complex issue and it's different for everyone. But here are a few things to consider.

### Money Is Taboo

Did you learn growing up that it is impolite to talk about money? That may be true in social settings but certainly not in business.

After all, we live in a capitalist culture! As a business owner, if you don't talk about money, then you can't ask for a client's budget or negotiate a contract. You can't raise your prices or advise a client that it's going to cost more when their project's scope starts to creep.

The fact is, clients appreciate it when you are straightforward about money. It conveys professionalism and confidence. Likewise, when you are cagey or avoid talking about money, it conveys amateurism and weakness.

That said, there is an art to talking about money. Sometimes it's appropriate to be direct about it; other times, it's best to put it in writing. The art is knowing the difference. (Much more about this in Part 2.)

## Money Is Emotional

Valterra writes, "Many of us are very conflicted about money in general—about having it, earning it and spending it. And many of us desperately don't want to think about it. Money should just be there, not interfering with how we live our lives. But we need it. And some of us hate that we need it."

In addition, creatives tend to practice "emotional pricing." That means quoting a fee based on nothing but a "feeling" and without calculating how much real time and effort is actually required. "They sit in a comfy chair, close their eyes, think about their work and say, 'Now what do I think I am worth?'" recounts Valterra. "And guess what—the number that pops into their heads is, on average, 20 percent lower than their true market value. Sometimes a lot lower."

Emotional pricing is not "wrong," it's just not rational. You have much more sophisticated tools at your disposal. Yes, be aware of what your gut says, but don't go only by your gut. When you make an emotional pricing decision and you realize later a better decision could have been made, take the time to investigate what drove you to make that decision so you can learn from those experiences.

## Money Conversations Are Minefields

Many creatives work alone. You may like it that way. You may need solitude or quiet to do your work. But business is social, and if you expect to earn a living then don't ignore the social aspect or you may find yourself in more solitude than you bargained for.

Money represents—and forces—an exchange with those other people, clients, colleagues, vendors and more. Talking money is one crucial aspect of business and rarely the smoothest part. There's usually some dissonance to deal with. You should expect that. Sometimes the client is shocked when you give your price, other times pleasantly surprised. Rarely are you "right on the money."

You may experience these exchanges as confrontations, but they are probably not as antagonistic as you may imagine. And if you welcome these exchanges and learn how to communicate ever more clearly, things are likely to go much more smoothly.

Kit Hinrichs, owner of Studio Hinrichs and longtime partner at Pentagram, says, "Money conversations are minefields because they tend to be emotional for both the creative and the client. Not knowing what to say can stir enough anxiety to prevent you from having the conversation at all."

If you're going to run a successful business, you have to be a clear communicator, especially when it comes to talking about money. Not only that, you need to be willing to stay in the conversation, through whatever discomfort arises, to keep the conversation going as long as necessary until each detail is resolved.

All of Part 2 is dedicated to those communications strategies. But first, complete the worksheet below to identify your personal obstacles to dealing with money.

## WHAT ARE YOUR MONEY ISSUES?

How much do you know about yourself and your money issues? Often, when we have trouble with an area of our lives, like handling money, we avoid thinking about it and end up perpetuating behaviors and situations that keep us from learning what can help us.

Unless we understand why we do what we do and where our behaviors and attitudes and beliefs about money come from, we are very likely to keep making the same mistakes. The way you first saw money handled at home may be the way you handle money now. Do you think your money issues benefit or hurt your business? If you can answer this question seriously you will learn to better assess your money issues and get one step closer to taking your business seriously.

So, here's our first step: Take some time to get to know yourself and money. Write one paragraph by answering as many of the questions as possible. (If you need more room, make sure some additional blank paper is handy.) Write the stories as memories you are recording in a journal entry. Spend fifteen minutes on each story. Think quickly and write fast.

### THE PAST: YOUR PERSONAL MONEY HISTORY

1a. Tell the story of how money was handled in your home.

What did you observe and experience about money? How was money talked about? With tension or with ease? Was it discussed in the open or was it never discussed? What family member was responsible for paying bills, going to the bank, balancing the checkbook? Did that person's behavior affect your money habits now? How did your family handle disagreements about money? How did your family come to resolutions about money?

1b. Money issues were handled calmly at home.

| Strongly disagree | Disagree | Not sure | Agree | Strongly agree |
|---|---|---|---|---|
| 1 | 2 | 3 | 4 | 5 |

2a. Tell the story of when you began earning money.

Did you get an allowance? When did you start working for money? What did you do with the money you earned or received? Did a member of your family teach you to save money? Did you save your money in the bank and not spend it? Or did you save it to have enough to buy something you wanted?

2b. I was taught good habits for handling money.

| Strongly disagree | Disagree | Not sure | Agree | Strongly agree |
|---|---|---|---|---|
| 1 | 2 | 3 | 4 | 5 |

## THE PRESENT: YOUR CURRENT MONEY STORY

1a. Tell the story of how you handle your money issues now.

Do you manage the money for your business? Do you manage your personal money? If not, are you confident in the person who does? Why or why not? What skills have you recently learned for handling money? What skills do you think are necessary for handling money?

1b. My money issues are handled calmly and confidently.

| Strongly disagree | Disagree | Not sure | Agree | Strongly agree |
|---|---|---|---|---|
| 1 | 2 | 3 | 4 | 5 |

2a. Tell the story of how it feels to handle your money now.

Are you organized, prepared and up to date? When unexpected money issues come up, do you feel anxious or confident? If you avoid money issues, why do you think this is the best plan? What do you do when confronted with stressful money situations? How do your money issues now compare with the way you as a child saw money issues handled in your home?

2b. My money issues are easy to handle.

| Strongly disagree | Disagree | Not sure | Agree | Strongly agree |
|---|---|---|---|---|
| 1 | 2 | 3 | 4 | 5 |

3a. What five things are you doing well in handling your money issues?

| 1. |
|---|
| 2. |
| 3. |
| 4. |
| 5. |

3b. What five things do you want to improve about your money issues?

| 1. |
|---|
| 2. |
| 3. |
| 4. |
| 5. |

3c. I am organized and confident about handling money issues.

| Strongly disagree | Disagree | Not sure | Agree | Strongly agree |
|---|---|---|---|---|
| 1 | 2 | 3 | 4 | 5 |

## YOUR ASSESSMENT SCORES

Assess your level of skill and commitment by totaling your score. What level is your result? Do you agree with your result?

5–11: Find help now

12–19: Learn more skills

20–25: Move to the next level

# WHERE YOU ARE NOW

Fill in the blanks below regarding your business income:

My goal is to make $ ___120,000___ a year. Today's date is _____. So far, I have made $_____ and I need to make $_____ more a month to meet my goal. Subtract $_____ for business and personal expenses, and I have made $_____ in profits.

# CHAPTER 2
# SETTING GOALS BEFORE PRICES

"I'm looking to grow in other ways by:

- increasing the quality of my relationships
- increasing my worth to my clients
- becoming a more efficient worker and business owner (while keeping a soft touch)
- identifying what is most enjoyable and/or lucrative

These aren't necessarily quantifiable goals, but they are guidelines to check back with."

**—KIRK ROBERTS,**
**PRINCIPAL OF KIRK ROBERTS DESIGN**

What do you want to achieve in your life? And how is your business one of the vehicles toward that goal?

If you haven't taken the time to define your own goals—from financial to lifestyle to lifetime achievement—then you probably don't have a plan in place to reach those goals. As the saying goes, "If you don't know where you're going, any road will take you there." Is that the road you're on?

Plenty of people run their businesses, and live their lives for that matter, without goals, but here's what happens: Without the framework provided by goals, you can end up overwhelmed by too many choices with no basis for making decisions. You won't know where to direct your business, which opportunities to seize and which to decline, which clients to take and which to let go, even which marketing activities are worth your time.

After all, we can't do everything. That's a fact. But without goals, you may try to. And it's likely you're being pulled in a million different directions if you haven't chosen the one that's best for you.

The alternative is simple: Think about where you want to go and outline the steps to get there.

Here's the secret: You may not reach your goals as set forth or it may take quite a while. But reaching them is not nearly as important as striving toward them.

## WHAT KIND OF GOALS ARE WE TALKING ABOUT?

"I want to earn $X." This is where many people start. For some, reaching a financial goal is a goal in itself.

But money can do so much more. It's best used as a tool to reach other goals. With it, you can buy time, afford a particular lifestyle, build all sorts of useful things, facilitate processes and give back. But not if you don't have enough even for yourself.

"What is my money for? What's important to me? How do I want to live? How do I want to spend my time? How have my priorities been determined?"

Maybe the problem is that you haven't taken the time yet to do that. Now's the perfect time.

It's your life, after all, and no one is forcing you to live it the way you do. If it's not working for you, change it. Setting goals can help. Ask yourself:

> "What do I value? What would my ideal work situation look like? Part-time work? Running a million-dollar operation? Freedom of schedule and freedom of place? Time to do what I enjoy? If so, what are those activities? How much vacation time do I want?"

Set up that vision, then create a business to support that.

What kind of business would allow that to happen? Is it a one-person shop that will allow you to work from home so you can spend time with your children while they're young? Are you aiming for a million-dollar operation that you can sell in ten years? Or a small studio or team of virtual partners working on high-quality, lucrative projects? There are so many options.

What will be your role? Do you want to always be doing the creative work, or do you want to learn how to manage others and bring in the business, which can also be very creative? It's challenging to do both, and that's where many creatives get stuck—not handing off responsibilities when doing so would allow the business to grow.

Here's how Janet Mobley of FatCat Strategies, based in Raleigh, North Carolina, envisions the growth of her business:

> "In five years, I want the business to operate as a full-service marketing department that becomes an indispensible extension of our clients' organizations. We'll have a stable of multi-year,

retainer-based relationships with small- to mid-sized, non-sexy local businesses."

"In order to deliver the services required, we need a few senior-level people and some number of entry-level people and interns to handle production work within each department. I would like to be doing mostly sales, new business development and helping with high-level account management."

Your goal might also be to become the "expert" in a specific field or industry. Eryn Willard of Thurmont, Maryland-based Studio 22, expresses her goal like this:

"I want to be the go-to firm for sustainability communications and outdoor recreation clients, and possibly merging the two."

## If Freedom Is Your Goal...

Freedom is one aspect of a lifestyle goal that comes up frequently among creative professionals, although it means something different for each. This is a dream for many but certainly within reach. It could mean the freedom to choose how you work and with whom; the freedom to work when and where you choose; or the freedom to be nimble and mobile, no matter what that means or how it manifests in your life.

Shawn Timen and Curtis Gorlich of Morning Sock Studios in South Carolina plan to run their design business from a thirty-foot sailboat that goes from port to port along the East Coast of the United States.

There are no right or wrong goals, of course. Least helpful are the general and abstract ones, which are easy to rattle off.

The real challenge is coming up with goals that are specific and measurable.

**Too general:** "Get more clients."
**Measurable:** "By December 31, I will have three new web projects at $20,000 each…"

**Too general:** "Make more money."
**Measurable:** "In third quarter, I will bring in a total of $20,000."

**Too general:** "Find work/life balance!"
**Measurable:** "By year's end, I will work no more than 50 hours per week."

Setting goals that are this specific could be a guessing game, especially if you are just starting out. But if you don't have a track record to draw on, go ahead and guess (that's all "corporate projections" are) and then adjust as your data is gathered.

Don't trick yourself out of setting goals by imagining you'll be too discouraged or frustrated if you don't reach your goals. What's important is having something to work toward and then measuring and analyzing when you fall short, which is very likely, especially at the beginning of this process.

With your goals in place, you are better positioned when opportunities arise to answer the question, "Will this get me closer to my goal?" If you can answer yes, then it's worth considering. If not, it's best to let it go so you can pursue something that will get you closer.

# SET YOUR GOALS

Once you decide you are ready to get serious, your next step is to look at the "big picture" goals you must set to create that success you want. Think about what you need most for your business right now, then fill in the blanks below.

One business goal I want to achieve:

*\* Gt 5 clients who pay me $90/h*

I will complete this goal by (date):

*End of January*

What might get in my way before I reach this goal:

*Not selling myself*

## BREAK DOWN YOUR GOAL

Brainstorm a list of five (or more) action steps that will get you to your goal. These are the steps you need to work toward each day. You won't know everything right away, so the steps should be a running list that you keep handy and continue building upon.

Here are some general steps that can be used to accomplish any goal:

1. Outline the objectives from beginning to end to complete your goal.

2. Estimate the time frame necessary to reach each milestone.

3. Draft a step-by-step plan to complete the objectives within your time frame.

4. Determine what help you need to complete each step.

5. Determine a budget for the money needed to reach your goal.

Now write down the steps you think will get you to your goal, and list them in order of priority. What needs to be done first? Then what? Then what? What's next? And so on…

| | |
|---|---|
| 1. | |
| 2. | |
| 3. | |
| 4. | |
| 5. | |
| 6. | |

## YOUR ACTION PLAN

Now you know what you have to do, so your next step is to turn your list of steps into a to-do list of specific actions. This is your action plan. Add the to-do list tasks and the completion dates to your calendar and start doing them today.

## YOUR FINANCIAL GOALS

Now let's focus on your financial goals for the next year.

Let's say your goal this year is to bring in total sales of $150,000 or $500,000 or $5 million. The first question that only you can answer is: Is that realistic?

That depends on where you start. If you've been in business a while and your total sales are, let's say, already $75,000, a 50 percent increase is ambitious but possible, especially if the economy is strong, if the market you've targeted is viable and if you're willing to work hard. On the other hand, if you just went out on your own, you have no clients yet and you're targeting a brand new market, it may not be realistic to go from zero to $150K so quickly.

Figure out what you'd need to do to get from where you are to where you want to go by choosing a number to measure against, such as an average fee per project.

For example, if you can charge an average of $25,000 for a website or publication, you'll only need six projects per year to reach $150,000. Those six—essentially one every two months—could come from six different clients, or perhaps you have three clients who each need two projects.

Likewise, if your average project is $5,000, you will need thirty of them, which is almost three per month, to reach the goal. How many proposals do you need to write to get thirty projects in a year? A standard that is used often is a 25 percent "hit rate." That means you win one out of every four proposals that you submit.

It is best to use your own experience as the yardstick. What is your average success rate with proposals? Do you get one out of four? One out of ten? Your own hit rate may be skewed if you aren't selective enough about which proposals you submit. The solution might be to say "no" more often so you can spend more time generating the right types of proposal requests.

What if your average project is small because your clients don't have a lot of money to spend? If all they can pay is $1,000, you'll need 150 projects to reach your goal. And how many prospects do you need to talk to before you actually sell 150? Is that realistic? The only way to find out is to try. You may discover you need to find a better market or to work more efficiently.

## MARKETING MAD LIBS

Not everyone you talk to will be a good prospect. So you need to figure out what percentage of live prospects you talk to actually convert to becoming clients. Is it one in twenty-five? One in a hundred? Then you figure out which combination of marketing tools you'll use to attract that many live prospects.

It may take you a year to figure this out with precision, or you may have a good sense after three or six months. This worksheet will get you started.

### FINANCIAL GOALS

My monthly financial goal is _____ .

When I look over past projects, I can see that the average amount billed per project is _____ . If I stay at this rate, I need _____ projects per month to reach the goal. [Or I need to get better projects, raise my rates, work more efficiently to boost productivity, etc....]

## PROPOSALS/ESTIMATES

Last month, I completed _____ proposals/estimates. The number of estimates that were accepted was _____ . This means my average acceptance rate is _____ .

Therefore, I need to generate _____ proposals/estimates per month to reach my monthly goal.

## GETTING THERE

To generate this number of proposals/estimates per month, I need to find lots of prospects. Here's how. Each week I will:

- Attend _____ networking events. (Try for once a week and choose ones at which you can meet at least ten new prospects each time.)

- Spend _____ hours per week on social networking. (If you're networking online where your prospects can see you, start with thirty minutes to one hour per day.)

- Comment on _____ blog posts in my target market. (Start with three times a week.)

- Write _____ blog posts for my own blog or someone else's. (Start with one per week.)

- Reach out to _____ new prospects via LinkedIn, e-mail, phone and snail mail. (Start with a number that's manageable to fit into your life, like two per day or five per week.)

## A BUDGET = GOALS + NUMBERS

A budget (from old French *bougette*, or "purse") is essentially a plan for your money. Literally, it is a list of all anticipated expenses and income (a.k.a. revenues) that is used for saving and spending.

Said another way: It's you telling your money what to do.

Many creative professionals run what looks like a successful business without a budget. And when things are running smoothly, all is well. But if you have goals to achieve, or equipment or maybe a building you want to buy, using a budget is the only way to get there. Without a budget, you're flying by the seat of your pants.

Of course, there are differences when it comes to budgeting for a "one person" operation vs. budgeting for a large company or firm. But no matter the size of your business, a budget can show you how your money is spent and earned. With a budget, you can see if, month to month, you are spending more or less than you anticipated, which will help you make a decision when the latest Apple gadget goes on sale. Instead of buying it just because everyone else is, you can consult your budget to determine whether the money is available, now or later.

## Scared of Budgets?

When your clients tell you what's in their budget, they're really saying, "I have a plan that allows for this amount of money to be allocated for this project." You should be able to do that too, no matter what size business you're engaged in.

See a sample budget at www.creative freelancerblog.com /money-guide.

If you had a regular paycheck, as most employees do, you would have no trouble deciding how much of that money to allocate to your fixed expenses, for example, and how much you can spend on optional expenses. What scares people about budgeting is actually not the budget itself. That's just a spreadsheet with harmless numbers. The scary part is the uncertainty of your financial situation.

You may not know how much you'll earn this year, or this month for that matter. That's when a budget becomes your friend, almost your protector. In fact, your budget will allow you to live with less stress during a time of uncertainty.

The more confident you are in your revenue projection for a given period of time, the less fear you should have of the budgeting process. But only if you know the numbers.

If you know, for instance, that you are assured only $3,000 worth of income next month, you may tighten your belt. The budget will be your plan for how to spend that money before the checks are deposited. Your budget can prevent you from spending more than you have coming in. Or, if you did, you would at least be doing it consciously. Without the awareness provided by the process of creating a budget, it's much easier to get yourself into financial trouble.

That doesn't mean that once you've created a budget it is set in stone. It's customary to revisit a budget plan to incorporate any new information. In the simple situation above, two weeks into the month you might attend a networking event and meet a prospect with a rush project. You get the job, and now your expected revenues are higher, perhaps much higher. You could leave your budget as is and consider it a good month.

But what if you keep up the networking and this happens every month? Is your budget as accurate as it could be? Probably not. The budget should be revisited and revised to align with the reality. By revising the budget, you make sure all expenses are properly accounted for and the revenue expectations are accurate. You might decide to take a larger salary or to buy that new gadget after all. This revised plan could also motivate you to spend more on marketing to generate even more business or to save cash to purchase equipment for planned growth.

## MAKING MONEY WITHOUT CLIENTS

### BY JENNIFER RITTNER

It seems both obvious and essential to recognize that there is no cookie-cutter solution to building a successful, sustainable business, let alone a successful ancillary revenue stream. The point is to find the path that makes the most sense for your particular set of skills and your business. Some things to keep in mind:

**Listen to yourself.** You know what you're good at. You know what you can handle. Be true to your own skills and capabilities.

**Listen to your audience.** Have clients, colleagues and friends asked for your handiwork, advice or services? If they are asking, maybe they (and others) would be willing to pay?

**Embrace risk.** You may have passion and expertise, but lack the confidence to implement new ideas. Take the risk to try something new and be rewarded, whether by the attention you garner, the potential revenue or the satisfaction of having completed something you feel passionately about.

**Be patient.** Give your new business venture time to work itself out, but don't get caught in a downward spiral. If it isn't making an impact (financially or creatively) within one to two years, it could be time to shut it down.

Enjoy what you do or make. Change happens best when it happens organically, as a natural outgrowth of your existing passion, expertise and interests.

**Make it relevant.** Timing is everything (and luck certainly helps). If you happen to capture the right idea at the right cultural moment, it will take on a momentum of its own. At the same time, you can position yourself to be aware and develop insight, not to manipulate and certainly not to follow trends, but to read the cultural landscape and discover when, where and how to contribute your own point of view to the conversation.

**Consider strategic partnerships.** You have allies in unusual places. In addition to finding collaborative opportunities with colleagues, you may discover some untapped resources, including sponsorship opportunities within your field—from vendors, industry partners and, occasionally, clients; investment money (for new product lines, innovation tools, etc.) from venture collaborations; or creative partners in complementary fields. But be wise about your partnerships, and always, always put it in writing.

**Believe in it.**

# CHAPTER 3
# SETTING YOUR PRICES

"I'm not charging enough, but I'm not convinced the market will bear a higher price. I have a pretty good idea how long it takes me to do a particular project; it seems there's no discernable method or "formula" for determining prices. I was frequently told I was too high—now I'm being told I'm too low. What to do?"

**—ANONYMOUS CREATIVE PROFESSIONAL**

There is no right "answer" when it comes to pricing. Rather, pricing is a process, and your prices should not be set in a vacuum or written in stone. The goal when pricing each project is to find the fees that fairly compensate you and that your client is willing to pay.

That's why no book—and certainly not this one—can tell you what your prices should be. That is something only you can determine, and ideally it should be done on a client-by-client, project-by-project basis. This chapter will offer some new ways to think about pricing so that you feel more confident discussing prices with clients.

As mentioned earlier, there is nothing objective to "what you're worth" and there's no way to figure out "what you deserve." Pricing creative services is notoriously slippery, with competitors across the country (and now around the world) willing to do a lot for very little. Sure, you can come up with a price based on what you need to earn or what a project is worth to you, but if that number doesn't fit with what your client can pay, the conversation won't go any further.

## WHAT EXACTLY ARE YOU SELLING?

Creative professionals spend an inordinate amount of time fretting over how much to charge. But there is no right or wrong price, often no "going rate" to fall back on. Instead, pricing is subjective and dependent on a wide variety of factors, including geographic location and timing, what the market will bear, the quality of the deliverable, the level of service and attention needed, how you've positioned your price in the first place (see Chapter 5, Positioning Your Price), even your level of desperation (hopefully low to non-existent), just to name a few.

Clear pricing is based on a clear idea of what you are really selling. You may believe that what you are selling—and what clients are buying—is time, and you therefore price by the hour. The problem is that as you get better at what you do, you'll spend less time and make less money. So if a twelve-page brochure used to take sixty hours and now it takes forty, do you charge less? Does that make sense?

What about the value of your years of experience, the effort you've expended developing your skills and talents, and your resulting expertise? What about the way you think? Your creative imagination applied to a client's specific problem? That has a value. It's not an objective value; in fact, it's highly subjective, which makes it challenging to quantify.

> What you are selling is peace of mind. It's your job to make your client comfortable and safe in the knowledge that you will take care of everything. If you do that, the good clients will choose you, even if you're the highest bidder.
>
> From *The Designer's Guide to Marketing & Pricing* by Ilise Benun and Peleg Top (HOW Books)

## THE FACTS ABOUT PRICING

To come up with a fair price for any project, you need to understand two things: the role price plays in your prospect's decision-making process and the elements that go into determining your price.

Often, your price is just one of many factors upon which your prospect will base a decision to hire you (or not). It is usually not the only factor and perhaps not even the most important one. In fact, it would behoove you to know how important it is in each case, and you should always ask.

Once you have the price in perspective, you can begin looking at the facts upon which it should be based. Those facts include how much time is required to do what needs to be done, plus how much you need to earn to run your business. If you're just pulling numbers out of the air based on your imagination (what you think they can or can't afford) and feelings (fear and hope are two big ones), then you won't know if what you charge will keep you afloat, and if you don't know, it's unlikely to do so for long.

You need to know:

**a. Your hourly rate.** Your hourly rate is very important to use for estimating purposes. It is not recommended, however, that you share that number with clients and prospects, although there are exceptions (discussed in more depth later in this chapter). This number, which you can calculate simply by dividing the hours you have available to work by your expenses plus profit, puts a value on the time you and your employees spend doing work that can be billed out.

For hourly rate calculation tools, go to www .creativefreelancerblog .com/money-guide.

**b. How long things take to do.** Tracking your time and putting a value on that time is a way to bring objectivity into what can be an otherwise subjective way of doing business. This is based on you tracking your time over weeks and months to find an average amount of time it actually takes to provide the main services you offer. You should know this, even as you get better and faster at what you do. You aren't directly charging for the hours spent, but you do need to know how much time is involved to ensure that your time is accounted for.

**c. What the competition is charging.** You need to know who your competitors are as well as what they are charging. It's not easy to find out. You can't exactly call and pretend to be a prospective client for them, although that is often what corporations do to gather this "intelligence." Do you have a network of colleagues with whom you can share this information confidentially? If not, you can always create one for yourself. Also, when you lose a project, you can ask about who was chosen and why, including what fees were quoted. (See Chapter

9: Confidently Closing the Sale, for details on what to say.) Even if you get general ranges, it's helpful.

You need to find out:

a. **Your client's budget range.** If you want to quote a price that doesn't cause sticker shock, you must try to find out what your client has in mind, at least a range. This is not always possible to find out and it often requires persistence. But it's well worth trying; otherwise you can waste a lot of time doing proposals you don't win. (For ideas on how to ask for this information, see Chapter 8: Talking Price and Negotiating.)

b. **The value of the project to your client.** When your customers buy creative services, they expect a return on their investment. Knowing their budget tells you something about the value they have in mind. If they're thinking $500 for something that you were going to quote $5,000 for, you can probably assume they don't put much value on the services, and you may not want to pursue the project unless you can persuade them of a higher value. This is also related to positioning your price. (Much more on that in Chapter 5: Positioning Your Price.)

c. **Other factors relevant to the decision-making process.** What does your customer care most about? It could be your depth of experience and familiarity with their industry. It could be the fact that you are actually one of their customers. They may value responsiveness and customer service over talent and creativity, with price being of less importance. Their most important factor could be something you have no control over, such as geographic proximity, and you might not know unless you ask.

## Value-Based Pricing

For more on value-based pricing, see www.creativefreelancerblog.com/money-guide.

More important than your price is the perceived value of your services to your prospect. Before a project, you must position your price by demonstrating the potential value you bring to them. If you can do this well, price will become irrelevant. Cameron Foote clarifies the concept of value-based pricing here.

## WHAT IS A PRICE?

### BY CAMERON FOOTE

It's easy to come up with a low price that pleases the client, and this is practiced every day by creatives around the world.

But the price is not the value. What is that project actually worth? What is the value of the project?

We all know that value, not price, is what clients should be concerned about. And you're better off with clients who know this. What they actually get for their money is the only true test of whether it's well spent.

Individuals often equate money with price. Much more appropriate would be to equate money with value. Value is the price in the context of the expected results. Whether your clients know it or not, value is much more important—and valuable—to the client.

The most important aspect of getting pricing right is the process of discussing all that clients will be getting for their money. Again, the idea is to make the conversation the core of the interaction, with price as just one of many variables to discuss.

But price, a fixed number, is much easier to fixate on. Value, often someone's subjective opinion, is much less attractive. We may like to talk about the "added value" that can come from working with us, but it is a claim that can easily lack substance when it goes beyond talent and creativity. What exactly are you promising when you talk about "value"?

Once you understand value, you will de-emphasize price. When you promise value—a reasonable price combined with outstanding results—you are speaking directly to both a client's real needs and your understanding of those needs.

Greater value does not have to be a promise of higher sales and greater market impact either, which you don't control and therefore can't promise. The value creators you *can* control and promise include faster turnaround, ease of working together and greater attention to detail, to name just three.

Your pricing has ramifications/effects well beyond the simple transaction between you and your client. The higher the price of any item or service, the more likely it will be appreciated and its producer respected. Firms need, of course, to be mindful that pricing does not exceed norms for their talent or their market. But just as important is recognizing that below-market pricing is usually suspect among knowledgeable clients. It cannot only result in losing projects from desirable clients, but it often damages a firm's quality reputation at the same time.

If you have employees, your pricing sends a message about the value of their talents, experiences and problem-solving skills. High prices raise employee morale; low prices lower it. (Example: "They've been giving my hard work away for practically nothing.")

Cameron Foote is editor of the *Creative Business* newsletter (www.creativebusiness.com).

## AN ARGUMENT FOR NOT CHARGING HOURLY

When asked about price, do you immediately answer with an hourly rate? And if so, is that the best way for you to price your services? It's worth some thought.

The point is not that charging by the hour is right or wrong. Everyone has to find the model that works best for them: by hour, by project or sometimes a combination of both.

The point is that if you quote hourly rates, you should know why you are doing it and whether you have alternatives. If you do this because that's the only way you can get hired by agencies, that's one thing. If it's a habit or the easiest way to work, then it may be time to try different approaches, such as project-based fees, retainers and even consulting arrangements. (More about this in Chapter 4: Pricing Strategies.)

The main problem with charging hourly is that the better you get at what you do, the less time it will take and the less you will officially be able to charge. In other words, you are not paid for your expertise but for your labor and nothing more. This is backwards and doesn't make sense in the world of creative services, where the more you learn, the better you get—and the more you should be able to charge.

Charging hourly may seem simple—all you have to do is track your time and multiply—but it actually causes a lot of stress. Inherent in charging hourly is the fear that you are taking too long and your client will not pay you for the time you will have already spent when it's all over. Most clients appreciate knowing your total fee. If they have $5,000 to spend for a brochure and you can finish it in an afternoon, what do they care as long as it's good?

According to Emily Cohen, consultant to the creative industries, "Calculating or negotiating fees based solely on hours estimated (and hourly rates) undercuts the importance of intangible value within our profession. In these cases, the client's perception of the [creative services provider] becomes that of 'service provider' or 'vendor,' rather than trusted expert—an expert who brings years of experience and industry insight to the relationship. Such expertise cannot be measured in hours or built into hourly rates."

## Exceptions to the Rule

As mentioned, none of this pricing process is as black and white as you might like it to be. There are times when charging hourly is best. It can inspire a chaotic client to be more efficient when they see clearly how their disorganization makes things take longer and cost more. Or, in an organization with many approval levels, using an hourly rate can either motivate those on a tight budget to move things along, or compensate you for the agony of too much non-constructive input.

There are also certain types of work or environments for which you have no choice but to charge hourly, such as:

- **Ad agencies or creative contractor agencies.** Charging hourly is standard practice if you're working through agencies, especially if you work on-site.

- **Corporate or government work.** Many government jobs require proposals written in hourly rates for auditing purposes. Some have a "design by committee" approval system, which takes longer and must be factored into a project fee if you don't charge hourly.

- **Revisions, maintenance, etc.** Charging hourly for revisions beyond the number of rounds agreed to in the original scope of work can help keep the project on track. Sometimes you need to show the client how much money they are wasting.

Once you've clarified the way that's best for you to price, you can begin to actually set your prices.

# CHAPTER 4
# PRICING STRATEGIES

"Working hard and waiting for things to fall in your lap rarely works. You get what you demand, not necessarily what you deserve. So start asking for what you want!"

**—MIKELANN VALTERRA, CERTIFIED FINANCIAL RECOVERY COACH AND AUTHOR**

Now that you understand how complex pricing can be and how much research, thought and interaction with the prospect or client is required, let's look at some actual strategies creative professionals use to price their services.

## IS THERE A "GOING RATE" FOR YOUR SERVICES?

For most creative services, the short answer is "no." It depends on so many factors, many of which were elaborated in chapter 3, including geography, budget, timing, etc.

Still, many have tried to codify that information, and it's important to be aware of what's out there, especially if you have no other basis for beginning to think about it. There are a couple of guides that are updated regularly to give you a sense of general price ranges, especially *The Handbook of Pricing and Ethical Guidelines*, published by the Graphic Artists Guild.

For more resources on pricing, see www .creativefreelancerblog .com/money-guide.

Keep in mind that what you find will only be "industry guidelines." In relation to the specific clients you are negotiating with, the prices suggested may seem too high or too low for the work you have in mind. You can use these guidelines to demonstrate to your client why you are charging what you are, which can be effective. If not, you're better off finding a price you can both live with, regardless of what "the industry" suggests.

## HOW TO FIND OUT THE "GOING RATE"

### BY MIKELANN VALTERRA

Is there a going rate for your services? Does it depend on your location, your depth of experience, your credentials or years at work? Sometimes, but not always.

You should always have a sense of the "fair market value" for what you do. You must do some market research to find this out. You can't guess. If you do, you'll probably guess wrong and probably too low. Finding out what others are charging can be a revelation. It provides objectivity where none was before, where a vacuum existed before. And it will help you put yourself and your services in perspective. You will probably be surprised at how all over the map the prices are, which means there is actually no "going rate." You'll find people with less experience charging more than you. Or someone whose work you think is inferior charging twice as much as you (and sometimes vice versa).

As you do your research, you will inevitably find a range. In fact, a range is what you are looking for. Once you are clear about the general range that people are charging for your type of service, you will have a better sense of where you fall in the range and what you can charge.

What if you set your rates on a day that you don't feel very good about yourself and your work? Doing research helps you to be objective about your rates.

If you do find something that resembles a "market rate," don't think it will stay that way forever. Rates can and do change, so keep your eyes open to see how. New competitors and new technology can greatly affect the market rate. A downturn in the economy can cause people to discount their prices, so where you were once in the middle, now you're at the top. New technologies like "crowdsourcing" may bring a flood of new, low-price alternatives to the market for your services, thereby threatening to devalue or diminish the value of yours, which means you either ramp up your marketing or adjust your pricing. Either way, it is important to stay in touch with what people are willing to pay.

Don't wait until it's time to raise your own rates to find out what the going rate is. You should always know the range of what people are willing to pay for your service.

Mikelann Valterra is a certified financial recovery coach and author.

## How to Research Your Rate

Beyond the industry guides cited above, there are people you can talk to and places you can go, especially online, to find out what others are charging and what you can charge.

### Ask Your Clients

The best resource for pricing information is your clients and prospects. They are the ones actually paying the fees and will know the going rate, if there is one.

This can be a delicate discussion, and it may not be appropriate to ask every single client. But there are probably a few with whom you have a strong relationship, who want to support the growth of your business and would be willing to share this information and perhaps much more. Do this over lunch or coffee (your treat!) and be ready with your questions to make it the most productive conversation possible.

### Ask Your Professional Colleagues

If another creative professional approached you at a networking event, engaged you in conversation and asked you all sorts of questions about your business, including what you charge and what's included in that fee, what would you say?

Of course it depends on the context and the person, but Mikelann Valterra suggests that there is nothing wrong with asking that question of the people you meet, too. She recommends phrasing it this way, "Hey Janet, can you give me a sense of your rates? I realized that I don't know." It's as simple as that.

Even better, be the first to offer. Be generous with details about your own pricing and the thinking behind it, even about your struggle to determine those prices. You may find you're not alone. And you're likely to learn quite a bit from each conversation.

If you feel more comfortable asking colleagues you know and trust, then find a small group you can join for the purpose of sharing information like this. And if you can't find it, start that group or network for yourself, either online or off. Claims Valterra, "Not only will you gain a lot of valuable information by asking these questions, but you will gain a deeper understanding of [your colleagues'] business and know when and how to refer to them."

### Scour the Internet

If you're looking for a less stressful way, you may be able to find some information online, although it may not be the most reliable source. A few of your colleagues or competitors might post a rate sheet, primarily to weed out the wrong prospects. Some trade associations make this information available as a benefit to their members, and some creative searching can turn it up. Try using keywords for the services you provide + "fee survey" or simply "rates."

## Options for Pricing Your Services

There are a few basic ways to price creative services.

**Time-based.** We've addressed pricing hourly, as many freelancers do and sometimes must. But for work that takes the time it takes, like strategic consulting, or that doesn't take less time the better you get, time-based options are worth considering. To make it worth your while, your hourly rate should be high and increase regularly with your growing experience and refined expertise.

You can offer short increments, fifteen minutes or a half hour, like lawyers do, or longer increments, such as a day rate, as consultants do. In fact, if you are looking to do more high-level, strategic work, it makes sense to try a consulting model and experiment with a day rate. If you've positioned your services well, clients will see the value and pay it.

**Project-based.** As discussed, this is the most common way to charge and it's especially useful when working with new clients. A project has a beginning, middle and end, which allows you to try a project with a new client to see what it's like to work with them, how much hand-holding is involved, how long the approval process takes, etc. Then you use that information when pricing the next project or the next phase in a more substantial project. In project-based pricing, time is only one element; you also factor in your overhead and your profit.

A subset of project-based work is "phased projects," where you price by phase. You can't price Phase 2 until Phase 1 is finished, as Phase 1 lays out the steps and specifics for Phase 2. This is a useful solution to pricing problems that arise when trying to price a substantial project with many unknowns, especially web design projects that can easily morph out of control. Pricing the phases separately means you're not locked into a price you devised when you necessarily knew very little, and it allows for lots of changes. The accumulated knowledge will be helpful in pricing later phases, and it will also help you avoid scope creep.

**Package-based.** More and more creative professionals are offering package deals, especially for clients with small budgets and, in particular, for web-related projects. A package price puts boundaries around a project that has no beginning, middle and end of its own. Whether you're offering writing or design services, you can create a package with X number of pages, X number of revisions and a variety of features included, all for a package price. Anything over and above gets charged as extra.

## Retainer-Based Pricing

For some creative professionals and firms, retainer arrangements are the ideal. The foundation of the agreement is that the client guarantees a certain volume of work over a certain time period. In exchange, the creative professional or firm completes that work for a fixed fee. This fee is usually based on hours accrued but can also be based on a set of deliverables.

Clearly, the steady cash flow of a retainer arrangement is a benefit—but when your fee is based on hours spent, be aware of the potential cost to your positioning. You may be perceived as just another vendor, instead of being valued as a strategic partner and for your experience as a creative. That's why value-based retainer arrangements focused on deliverables—the scope of work done—are better for you. (Exceptions to that rule exist, of course, such as when you're doing maintenance on a website.)

That's one reason why retainer arrangements work best for strong, existing relationships. It can be a natural progression from project-based work with a client that values your work. Don't try it out with a client you've never done business with, as you won't know the subtleties of that relationship until you're in it for a while. Spend six months, at least, working on a project basis first.

As for structuring a retainer arrangement, Emily Cohen says, "Retainers based solely on hours accrued are best used for implementation and/or execution-level engagements." She suggests that a better way to structure a retainer, especially for strategic, conceptual-level relationships, is to define it instead against a scope of work. That way, it is based on value, not time, and negotiated on defined deliverables, not hours accrued. "You agree to complete X number of projects throughout the year and you get a monthly fee for that. So the 'retainer' is actually a payment plan for a scope of work. You can discount your rates if you like but you're not going to return any money for time that is unused. And you accomplish your goal, which is steady cash flow."

A retainer agreement is a commitment and should be no shorter than six months, but it can be a one-year contract that extends, if all is working well. Use the contract renewal milestone to discuss and modify the arrangement as needs change—yours and theirs. That, in itself, will help keep lines of communication open.

## RETAINER Q&A WITH EMILY COHEN

**Q:** What is a retainer arrangement?
**A:** To a client, a retainer arrangement is when a creative professional or firm provides discounted fees in exchange for a commitment to ongoing work and regular cash flow. They usually expect priority attention and quick turnaround.

**Q:** What is necessary for a retainer arrangement to work well?

**A:** Retainer arrangements tend to work when there is open communication and clarity about what each side is giving and getting, as in any consensual agreement.

**Q:** What are the problematic issues to be aware of?
**A:** First of all, most retainers are based on a certain number of hours you allot to the client. But what happens if they don't use those hours? Do you return them? Do they roll over? And if so, for how long? All of this needs to be discussed and negotiated. A trial period can help, where you agree to something, try it out for three months, then assess and discuss whether adjustments need to be made.

**Q:** What are the benefits to the creative professional?
**A:** It's a bit less paperwork and time saved because you don't have to spend hours working on proposals. That will often justify the discounted fees.

**Q:** Any best practices?
**A:** You should keep (and submit to the client) a summary of what has been accomplished each month. These arrangements have lots of gray areas, so they need to be entered into seriously, with clear guidelines and processes for regular and clear communication.

Emily Cohen is a consultant to the creative industry (www.emilycohen.com).

## Sample Retainer Arrangement

Sharon Bending, of Chicago-based Bending Design, has retainer relationships with a few of her clients in the financial services and association industries. Here's how she structures them:

- **Time frame:** The client must commit to a minimum of six months and a minimum of ten hours per month. Any less than that and it's hard to get anything accomplished; you'll spend more time checking your time than getting work done.

- **Payment:** We agree to a set number of hours ahead of time and they pay that full amount before the month begins because I have to set aside those hours. The client is charged an hourly rate, which is a benefit because normally we charge by the project.

- **Prioritizing the work:** I set the schedule of work as much as possible in a weekly call to review priorities. Otherwise they are likely to throw work at us and expect everything to be done at the same time.

- **Reporting:** They get a report of the hours, including descriptions, at month's end so they can evaluate if they need more. (I don't even think my clients read this, but they feel better knowing you are doing it.)

- **Overage:** If we are running close on hours, I let them know, and I always get their permission before going over. If we go over on hours, they're billed at a higher hourly rate.

## A WORD ABOUT MARKUP

It is customary in business to charge a markup, that is, an additional fee for outside services you purchase for a specific project. Unfortunately, many creative professionals don't feel comfortable charging this fee or fear their client won't agree to pay it.

The rationale behind this markup is sound: When bringing outside resources to a project, you use not only your skills and talents but also your time, expertise and your existing relationships with vendors, for which you need to be compensated, not to mention the time required to negotiate the services needed, then to manage that aspect of the project. You should not be doing that for free.

*Creative Business* newsletter has surveyed subscribers and found that, "markups on most outside items and services (delivery charges, service bureau fees, other creative services and miscellaneous materials) range from 15 to 30 percent, with the single most common markup being 25 percent. Markups on printing, however, are often an exception due to higher costs and greater risk."

## TRACK YOUR TIME
## TO CALCULATE PROFITABILITY

No matter how you price your work, time is a critical factor, whether you reveal your hourly rate or not. So it's essential that everyone's time is tracked, from principals of creative firms to all interns and freelancers. Not only will this help calculate accurate profitability, it will also make staff- and process-management much clearer. Instead of guessing who's doing what in how many hours, you'll know.

Go to www.creative freelancerblog.com /money-guide for recommendations of handy gadgets and cool tools for tracking time.

The stumbling block, of course, is making people do it, including yourself. It can be challenging to develop a time-tracking habit, but that's all it is—a habit. And there are many handy gadgets and cool tools to make it practically painless, but you have to use them.

If you do track your time, here are the benefits as outlined by Emily Cohen: "Time should also be recorded daily for improved accuracy; weekly time tracking is ineffective and ultimately just a guess. A firm that calculates profitability based on accurate time tracking and realistic hourly rates is better prepared to:

1. keep historical financial records for past projects that can then be used to determine pricing for future projects of similar value, scope and complexity;
2. identify profitable relationships and projects;
3. identify and eliminate unprofitable relationships and projects."

### Perfectionist, Heal Thyself

Creative professionals are notorious for over-servicing their clients. You love the creative process and want to do your very best—it's a point of pride—so you finesse every last detail and stay up way too late to finish a project. A common way to lose money—especially if you are a perfectionist—is to spend too long on projects that don't pay enough.

Unfortunately, most clients can't tell the difference between mediocre and excellent design. That's why you must know when you've spent the allotted time, when what you've produced is "good enough" and when it's time to move on to the next paying project.

Going the extra mile once in a while, whether the client notices or not, is fine and can even add value to your business. It's very gratifying when clients recognize and appreciate the polish you bring to your work, especially if that appreciation comes in the form of a premium fee. But if you're regularly spending 20 percent more time on every job—which you'll know if you track that metric—it may be time to rethink things.

## RAISING (AND LOWERING) YOUR RATES

Prices go up but hardly ever down. So it's expected that where your prices are today isn't where they will stay forever. But many creative professionals are still charging the same prices as when they started, or not much more. Are you?

If so, it may be the fear that your clients just won't pay one penny more than they currently pay. That may be the truth for your current crop of clients.

It may also be that you don't know how or when to raise your prices. Here is one approach.

Ideally, you should be earning more every year, not because you are so wonderful that you "deserve" more, but because you are perfecting your craft and learning more every year. Therefore, what you provide is worth more. As your business grows, as it naturally will, you evolve from one type of client to another, from one type of project to another, constantly reaching for better (sometimes bigger) clients and projects. That means you grow out of current clients and reach toward better ones. Leaving behind what doesn't fit anymore is a natural part of any life cycle.

With this mind-set you can consider each new client an opportunity to raise your rates—just a little. Add 5–10 percent to what you charged last time for a similar project and see what happens. Try it as an exercise. This way, no existing client is affected by the increase but—all things being equal—you get the benefit of earning more every year. It's a flexible way to price, especially if you're just starting out, when you're likely to price too low anyway. Get in the habit of doing this and it will become easier each time. (One caveat: If you're not organized, it can become complicated, as you have to track what you're charging to whom.)

## Raising Your Rates With Existing Clients

Don't worry. This approach doesn't mean that you have to give up the "old" clients you like. Some will stay with you and those who do will need to be trained to expect an increase, perhaps every other year or according to other milestones. For example, certain seasons or times of year are conducive to change and can be used as a catalyst, such as the new year. Anything new, for that matter, can serve as a justification for increasing prices: new company name or business structure, new office, equipment or employees.

You can move long-term clients slowly and incrementally toward a higher rate. What's important is setting the precedent that things will change—the specific change is incidental. So even if the increase is miniscule, what's important is that it takes effect.

Or you can suggest a different type of working relationship with an existing client. For example, if you've been working hourly to date, you can suggest moving to project-based fees. When you modify or upgrade your services is a perfectly logical time to increase prices too, especially for existing clients. Offering new services is like a new beginning. It creates a new mind-set, especially if you position and promote it that way. Old rules no longer apply, and the result is much less push-back from existing clients.

Often, in fact, negative reactions to higher prices are a result of how they're presented, not the prices themselves. Always give clients plenty of advance notice that something new is coming up. Give them details about how they will be affected. Give them time to respond and an opportunity to provide feedback.

Inevitably, some clients will fall away as you increase your prices, while others may decide to stay on because the value you provide is greater. You also might be tempted to use a rate increase to get rid of clients you actually want to fire. This is not a great strategy because it doesn't always work. They may just accept your increase and then you're still stuck with them.

Instead, it's better to advise a client that your business is growing. You don't need a lot of explanation. Emily Cohen suggests saying,

> "We've outgrown each other and I'd like to recommend someone else who can help you."

That way, you don't abandon them, but you aren't tethered to them for the rest of your days. This is also something that gets easier with practice.

## Lowering Your Rates

In difficult economic times, many businesses lower their rates and modify their services; they make concessions and negotiate with clients in order to get the work that's there. There is nothing shameful about any of this, if you do it the right way.

The guideline to use is this: Don't do it just because someone balks at your first price. And only do it when you adjust the services offered as well.

That said, there are situations in which a discount is standard procedure or a useful technique to achieve a different goal. For example, you can regulate your cash flow by offering an early pay discount to institutional or corporate clients who would otherwise take their sweet time to pay. But it doesn't always work.

According to Cameron Foote, "With many clients, early-pay discounts are not necessarily a guarantee of speedy payment and it is not unknown for some to take the discount and still pay on their regular schedule. So offering an early-pay discount could be just giving money away. A usual exception, though, is large government and institutional clients. In many cases they are mandated, either by law or their own procedures, to pay any invoice that offers a discount first. Although 2 percent off if paid within ten days (written as 2% 10/net 30) is typical, any early-pay discount usually moves an invoice to the top of their pile."

Whenever possible, before you lower your prices, offer instead to add something in exchange for the proposed price. In some cases the same end is achieved but you haven't cheapened the perception of your services. Instead, you've actually added value and held your ground. It's worth trying.

## SEVEN WAYS TO MAKE MORE MONEY

### BY MIKELANN VALTERRA

1. You can raise your fees and charge more.

2. You can increase your number of clients and therefore bill more hours. (This means putting in more time.)

3. You may be able to leverage your time by selling it in ways besides working for private clients (for example, you can offer groups or seminars).

4. You can hire staff and either bill their time for more than you pay them or use their help to work with more clients.

5. You can subcontract work that comes to you and make money on commission or earn the difference between what you pay the subcontractor and what you collect from the client. (This is similar to point number 3.)

6. You can earn referral fees or finder's fees by referring prospects to other creative professionals who offer complementary services.

7. You can create and sell products, thereby diversifying your revenue and having more than one stream of income.

Mikelann Valterra is a certified financial recovery coach and author.

# CHAPTER 5
# POSITIONING YOUR PRICE

"The appearance of prosperity increases the odds of landing projects and keeping clients. Equally important, it has a direct effect on how much clients will be willing to pay. (Think of it this way: Lord & Taylor can charge more than Wal-Mart). To attract and fly with eagles, you have to look and act like an eagle."

**—CAMERON FOOTE, EDITOR OF
THE CREATIVE BUSINESS NEWSLETTER**

True story: Dave's new prospect had what sounded like a big, juicy project, with the potential for ongoing work. He'd spent two hours meeting with his prospect, had established a good rapport and was confident he could do a good job. They asked him to submit a proposal. He asked for their budget. They said they didn't know. He went back to his office to work out his fees.

The fee he came up with was the highest he'd ever charged. But this was a big job. Dave had consulted industry pricing guidelines and was well within the standard range.

When he presented the proposal, the client "flipped out" about the high fee. The client had received proposals from other creatives and wanted to know how Dave's work, even if it is exceptional, could be worth double what the others were proposing?

There is no good way to answer this question when a prospect asks it at this point in the process. It's too late. If you don't set the groundwork that prevents this question in the first place, this is exactly what happens.

But what happened, exactly? Dave didn't position his price. He didn't prepare the client for what was coming. He'd gotten his client excited about the project without setting the stage for what it would cost. When the client flipped to the page in the proposal with the numbers, as most clients do, they "flipped" themselves because it wasn't what they expected.

What were their expectations? That's what this creative professional should have found out in advance.

Whether prospects have found their way to you or you've proactively pursued them, your first job is to find out if there is a fit between you. Do you have the skills and the knowledge that best serves their needs, and is there a financial fit? Can they afford you? If not, you'll waste a lot of time in conversation or, worse, writing a proposal that will be rejected.

With that question top of mind—*Is there a fit?*—do a little research. Look at similar projects they've done and evaluate the quality in terms of the going rate for work of that caliber. Or, better yet, see who did it. One of your competitors? An unknown? It doesn't take long to assess whether someone is used to paying a decent buck for work—or not.

## HOW TO PREVENT STICKER SHOCK

Once you feel comfortable that there is a fit, you begin the process of positioning your price—establishing credibility and demonstrating your professionalism—so that when you eventually present your price, there is no sticker shock.

How to prevent this unpleasant occurrence? Communication. You must communicate—visually as well as verbally—the quality and substance of your service offering so that your client's expectations adjust to align with your actual pricing, before you present your prices.

Think through and design absolutely everything you do with the goal of providing context and setting a strong foundation for your price. Without that context, clients can only compare one price to the next. It's your job to give them enough information to know the difference between your price, which may be higher but brings more value, and your competitor's.

How do you do that?

Everything you do, say and show, no matter the medium, must support and buttress your eventual price. This includes the obvious online and offline marketing materials, from your website and social marketing activities to the collateral materials you send in response to an inquiry and any tools you use to position yourself as an expert.

Strong presentation materials differentiate you and build your brand, while attention to dress and demeanor—stylish yet professional—convey more than you may imagine about what you should be paid. Continuous marketing reinforces awareness and familiarity, thereby building trust. Those are givens.

Consider also how you handle each interaction, from the conversation in which you scope out the project and the presentation of your proposal tailored to their needs, to the selection of appropriate references to say wonderful things about you and the diligent way you follow up. Through the entire process, you are offering a taste of the experience of working with you or your firm, conveying the professionalism and authority that will support a higher price.

But that's merely the superficial positioning. There's also...

## Your Confidence

You are the expert when it comes to doing your work, even if you can't claim to be the "expert" in a particular field. Don't assume they know more than you do about what they're asking for. Your prospect usually knows a lot less about the work they need than you do.

From the very first exchange, take the lead with confidence and pre-empt questions about price whenever possible. For example, in the initial conversation, you can say,

> "Here's how we usually handle this type of inquiry. Tell me everything you can about your organization and the project. I'll do the same, providing some relevant background based on what I learn. Then we can talk through the overall scope and the steps we might take to achieve your goals. And we'll make sure we both have the same picture in our heads of what this project is trying to accomplish and where it fits into your big picture before we talk price."

You've automatically pushed the price to the end of the conversation, giving you a chance to position your price.

## Your Credibility

Credibility comes in many forms, from testimonials in the words of satisfied (and if possible, impressive) clients, to credentials bestowed by industry groups.

You also imply credibility through specific "thought leadership" marketing tools, such as:

- case studies of relevant experience posted on your website and published in white papers
- announcements of awards through press releases and social media
- speaking engagements at industry trade shows
- being quoted in articles or, better yet, writing articles that position you or your firm as a leader in the field

That's all general credibility. You must then bring your credibility to bear on the specific client and project. Once again, this happens by engaging your client in conversation about their goals so you can respond with stories about relevant experience that demonstrates your knowledge. It doesn't have to be all "success stories" either. You can tell stories about the lessons you learned when mistakes were made and corrected. That makes you more real.

## Your Questions

The biggest mistake creative professionals make is not asking enough questions and not asking the right questions. The obvious reason to ask questions is to get the answers you need to assess your fitness for a project and to provide an accurate price.

But much more important than those answers is the effect of your questions on your prospect. The questioning process is a positioning activity, a chance to demonstrate what you know, to identify your specific value to the project and to show that you are more than "just a creative"—that you are a business professional who can think strategically and who takes the job seriously.

The client may not answer all of your questions. But the fact that you ask thoughtful questions speaks volumes about how you work and can be the difference between winning and not winning a project.

## TRUE STORY: "WE CHOSE YOU FOR YOUR QUESTIONS"

Maya Kopytman of C&G Partners responded to a request for proposal (RFP) for a six-figure web design/development project for a higher education institution. At first glance, the RFP was vague and confusing so she went through the RFP line by line and came up with more than twenty questions to submit during the formal question period.

Some of her questions pointed out contradictory requirements from one page to another. "I caught them being inconsistent. 'On page 15 you say X and on page 13 you say Z and that doesn't make sense. What do you mean?'"

Through thoughtful questions, Maya's firm not only demonstrated how well they understood the process they were being asked to bid on (and that they'd taken the time to actually read the entire RFP) but also showed the client how much help they needed from an expert, thereby identifying the value the firm brought to the process. "My questions triggered answers that actually doubled the scope of the RFP and I priced it high."

"When they issued the official answers, I could see the other vendors' questions and all of the answers, which gave me a peek at the competition. You can usually tell from the style of the questions how many you're competing against. Eighty percent of the questions were mine. The rest were very superficial questions, indicating to me that the others hadn't quite read the whole RFP. That encouraged me to proceed."

"In the end, we won it, and my hunch was confirmed. We were one of three firms competing, and the other two were quite formidable. When we were awarded the project, the client told us they had a predisposition toward us because of the thoroughness of the initial questions. In fact, we helped them shape the project through our questions. They said, 'We applaud you on your proposal because it covered every single point in the RFP and you answered all the questions we had before we could even ask them.'"

### Which Are the Right Questions to Ask?

If questions are so important, how do you know which ones to ask?

Go to www.creative freelancerblog.com /money-guide for examples of a new prospect questionnaire.

Many successful creative professionals have developed a questionnaire to use with new prospects.

This tool not only does its job by gathering information but also conveys professionalism and order—just because you took the time to create it.

So what questions should you be asking your prospects? Start with these:

1. "How did you find me (or us)?"

Did they find you on the web or through marketing you've done? Through a referral or some other word-of-mouth? They may not remember, but this is important information to try to collect. It can tell you which of your marketing tools are working best.

💬 2. "Why did you call me (or us)?"

Was it something they saw on your website? Something specific they heard about you? If you can find out exactly what it is that drew them to you, that may indicate what's important to them, giving you an edge over the competition.

💬 3. "What do you think you need?"

Your prospects and clients may not know what they need but you should begin by getting a sense of what they think they need. Together, you may discover needs they never knew they had. But if you don't ask them what they think they need, you may never discover that either.

💬 4. "What are your goals for this project?"

At this point, you're looking for high-level objectives, including target audience and primary competitors. Don't get into too much strategy or depth yet. That level of discovery and planning is what they will pay you for, but you must foreshadow the type of value you can bring. You can elaborate once they define the scope of work.

💬 5. "Why are you doing this now?"

Whether a website, annual report or brochure, find out what is triggering it. Do they need customers right away? Are they merging with another company? Have they lost a partner and need to make some changes? All of this will influence how you think about what you're going to propose and how you price it.

💬 6. "What's the deadline or time frame?"

Of course, you want to know when they need the project finished, which will affect the price. Are the timelines realistic? Aggressive? If so, and they acknowledge it, you can talk about what it will take to get it done within their time frame, such as getting freelancers or staff to work on the weekend, or buying some rush time at the printer. Then estimate accordingly: "Here's what it costs to do what you're asking. Will it cost less if we can get another week? Yes. Let me recalculate and get back to you."

💬 7. "Who is our competition?"

A lot of creatives resist asking this, perhaps assuming the client won't say. And sometimes they won't. But sometimes they will, and it will help a lot if you know. Veteran designer Petrula Vrontikis says, "If a prospect tells me that they are talking to the other two top branding firms in L.A., I know I can price higher because I know what they're getting from the others. Whereas, if they tell me the other option is their nephew, that also tells me how (or whether) to price." Also ask if they're talking to firms they've worked with in the past—which are easily searched even if they won't name them. Even if they won't give you names, it's important to know whether they are talking to other people or if they're already sold on you and are simply finalizing the details.

💬 8. "What is your selection criteria?"

How will they select and which factors are important to them? Also, ask about their approval process. How many stakeholders will review and approve the work you present? If it's more than your contact, you'll want to include plenty of positioning in your proposal for those who know nothing about you yet.

9. "Who is the decision-maker?"

You want to know who is making the final decision on the project, and you may want a certain level of contact with that person as well. Some creative professionals are adamant about this and won't take on a project if they can't meet with the final decision-maker from the beginning. Others aren't as rigid about it. In fact, you may not want the decision-maker—often the CEO or member of an executive committee—in the room for the nitty-gritty. The point is to judge whether your contact has a direct line to, and the trust of, the decision-maker. Making that call requires instinct honed by the right questions. You don't ask outright, "Do you have the power or not?" Instead, ask how their decision process works. Ask these questions with caution, lest you sound like you're asking them to prove that they're viewed from above as trusted counselors.

Start with diplomacy and practice the art of asking questions that will steer the client toward the answers you need.

"Does so-and-so like to be included at this stage? I'd be happy to come back and meet with her as well."

"How do you like to involve so-and-so in these kinds of projects? Are you confident that she has had time to think through what she is looking for, so we know we're heading down the right path?"

It's a matter of style. Part of the questioning process is finding yours. As you gather information, ask for the names of all the employees who will be involved in the process and their roles. If your contacts are not immediately forthcoming, ask about individual tasks associated with the project and how they will be handled, by them or by you. That usually gets them talking about the team.

## TWENTY QUESTIONS
## TO ASK BEFORE YOU DO A PROPOSAL

Here's a more comprehensive list of questions to choose from, based on the project at hand:

1. What are your goals for this project?

2. What are your expectations for the proposal? What would you like to see in it?

3. What would you like to see during the proposal presentation?

4. Do you have a budget set for this project? If so, what is it?

5. Do you have an overall marketing budget set for the year? If so, would you feel comfortable sharing that information?

6. What is your timeline for this project? When are you hoping for it to be completed?

7. Do you have someone in mind for the project already, or are you actively looking for new vendors?

8. Who will be the main point of contact?

9. Who will be the decision-makers on this project? Will they be involved at every step in the process?

10. How much time will your team need to make decisions in between drafts?

11. If this is a rush, will you/the team be available on evenings/weekends for review?

12. What is the driving force behind your firm selection? Price? References? Past work?

13. Do you know what you're looking for in terms of the overall direction, or will you "know it when you see it"?

14. Do you anticipate being able to stick to the schedule and provide feedback and necessary items when scheduled, or do you think you might run late given other factors?

15. Are you also looking for other assistance or services?

16. Will you provide all the text/content for the various projects?

17. How many other firms are you talking to? What is their approximate size?

18. Have you worked with creative professionals in the past? If so, who are they?

19. What was your experience working with other creative professionals?

20. Is there a creative professional that you are currently working with that you will be comparing our services to or looking to replace? If so, why?

## Your Process

Walking and talking your prospect through your creative process is one more way to show your expertise. Even if a description of your process is posted on your website or even if you think it's the same as everyone else's, take the time to describe how you work, from your creative methods to your billing procedures.

Why? Having a process implies extensive experience—"We've done this many times before"—as well as a sense of order, counteracting the bad rap creatives often have of being "flaky."

Describe in detail how you work, with an emphasis on your client's role in the process and what your expectations would be of them. You sound like you know what you're doing—because you do. This builds trust and confidence.

You are educating your clients and prospects not only about how you work but perhaps even about the general process of working with a creative professional. Note, however, that this education should be in no way patronizing. Be attentive to your tone. It shouldn't feel to them like they're being lectured. It's more about putting them in your shoes. The approach is, "Let's talk about how this is going to work from our perspective. As you know, this has to happen…" then go into as much detail as they seem to have the interest in.

Not describing your process in detail is like submitting a two-page estimate for a six-figure project. It is insubstantial and, worse, leaves a vacuum for the prospect to fill with what they imagine—rather than asking questions to make sure they have the right answers.

Guiding your prospect through your process is especially important when you don't have specific experience in the type of project they're offering. Show how your proven approach and past experience aligns with their particular needs. Say it with confidence—don't blink. (Unless you don't actually think you can do it. In which case, why are you there?)

From the client side, Dana Manciagli of Microsoft agrees, "Your clients perceive you as more professional, organized and 'buttoned up' if you have a clear process and approach. They will have more confidence that you will come in on-budget and on-time if you present your disciplined approach early on."

### Defining the Scope of Work

Defining the scope—the specific needs and parameters of a project—is the core of your positioning process. It's your chance to support the price you intend to propose for the work. As with any good conversation, you should frame the scope of work so that your prospect has an investment, a role to play in the collaborative process. You can even say,

> "We're working with you to define the scope of work so we can get you a firm price you can hang your hat on."

Take the general process you've already described and make it relevant to them, building a deeper bond and identifying your value to this project as you ask more questions, as you learn more and as you help them define or clarify their goals. Focus on their needs and your understanding of their needs. Maybe you can identify a need they weren't aware of in the first place, or find points in the process where they might get tripped up, which you would know because you're the expert—again highlighting your value and expertise, implying, "You really should not do this without us."

Through this conversation, you've created a bond such that the prospect realizes he needs you. Not until it is clear what you have to offer, not until you've identified where you can add something the client will value, should you start giving firm prices.

## Your Proposal

It goes without saying that a detailed proposal document is an important positioning tool, especially if you're pursuing complex projects from large organizations. But many creative professionals, especially those who shy away from "selling," tend to use the proposal to do the bulk of the selling. But it can't. That is not its purpose.

Instead its purpose should be to demonstrate your thinking process and your creative process, in both words and images, as you outline your approach and strategy, giving even more of a taste of what it would be like to work with you. It should provide details about any background and experience that is relevant to the project.

Either way, remember this is all part of marketing and positioning and it will represent you in your absence to strangers who are trying to compare apples to apples. You can safely assume your proposal will be used to sell your services up the chain to management and other stakeholders you don't even know exist. Never assume they'll have been brought up to speed on earlier conversations, e-mails, etc. Those people won't have spoken to you or met you. They won't have seen your website. Don't assume the positioning you've taken such pains to set down will flow through to them. It's possible that all they have is your proposal. So if you wonder whether to include an idea that was discussed during your conversations or additional samples you already showed to your direct contact, go ahead and include them. Make sure your proposal presents the full picture of your services and makes the strongest and most complete argument possible for why you are the best candidate for the project.

The positioning carries all the way through to the actual prices you quote, which should be round numbers. For example, quoting $10,000 conveys confidence and aligns with "value-based pricing" rather than something that looks like a result of calculating hours, such as $9,553.

Also, many proposals are filled with mostly generic material that gets recycled from one proposal to the next, often conveying heft rather than substance.

Yes, you need a template for your proposals so you don't have to reinvent the wheel each time you create one, but to be effective as a positioning tool, the proposal you submit should be anything but generic. Once you've gathered all the information that leads up to this part in the process, customize your proposal so that it reads like a document written expressly for them. Include as many details as you can and references to conversations you've had. Go out of your way to think through the project and let that thought process be reflected in the document. You might even include additional research you've done.

See some sample proposals at www .creativefreelancerblog .com/money-guide.

In situations in which you have no contact with the actual prospect, as with an RFP, you must also take pains to reflect back exactly what the prospect is asking for and looking for. (See more about RFPs in Chapter 13: Requests for Proposal.)

That's why it's recommended to hire a professional writer or consultant to write or at least review your proposals. There should be more than one set of eyes on it.

---

## NO SURPRISES

### BY CAMERON FOOTE

Every client should have, or be given, a rough idea of how much things cost before an estimate or proposal is put on the table. It vastly improves the odds of acceptance. For general inquiries, this is easily accomplished by providing a "How I (We) Work" sheet, or by verbally giving a high-low range for representative projects (a 100 percent spread). Either will disqualify tire kickers without discouraging real prospects. A verbal 100 percent range is also appropriate for inquiries on specific projects.

When preparing proposals whose price might come as a surprise, give a heads-up. For instance: "I wanted to alert you before our meeting that we are probably talking somewhere around $X." Alerting them poses some risk, but it is preferable to sticker shock at a presentation, and it will provide time to make any necessary adjustments.

Cameron Foote is editor of the *Creative Business* newsletter (www.creativebusiness.com).

---

### Your Proposal Presentation

If your proposal is going to be effective, your prospect has to look closely at what's in it, even read it. Unfortunately, most clients collect a stack of proposals, skim them (often online), look at the pictures (if there are any), then flip (or scroll) directly to the page with the numbers.

One way to guarantee that they read it thoroughly is to walk (or talk) them through your proposal in real time. This is an important aspect of using the proposal as a closing tool and it is your very best opportunity to get the job.

Remember that your proposal is one part of a conversation, and you need to be present for the response. Your prospects need to understand what you have to offer and how you are different from your competitors. Don't make your proposal shoulder that burden. You can do a much better job in real time and through direct contact.

Arrange to present your proposal in person. To get them to agree to this, start laying the groundwork early in the process. At the end of your very first meeting or phone call, instead of saying the usual, "We'll get back to you with a proposal," say,

💬 "When can we meet to go over the proposal?"

That question implies that this is your standard process.

If they say, "Just send it to me," respond with:

💬 "We want to have the opportunity to explore points further with you in real time, so we'd appreciate the chance to present it in person [or on the phone]."

While an in-person presentation is best, if they are not local, a phone presentation is a good solution. Go on to emphasize the benefits of presenting the proposal this way, such as:

• They will have a chance to ask questions about anything unclear and to correct anything that was misunderstood.

• If the proposal needs to be revised based on new or clarified information, it can be discussed as part of that meeting, thereby saving valuable time and bringing the proposal closer to what they actually need.

So you've started adopting the business mind-set, you've set some goals and begun to shift your thinking a bit about how to price your services and position that price. You're ready for Part 2. It's time to practice talking about it with real prospects and clients.

# PART TWO

# HOW TO TALK ABOUT IT

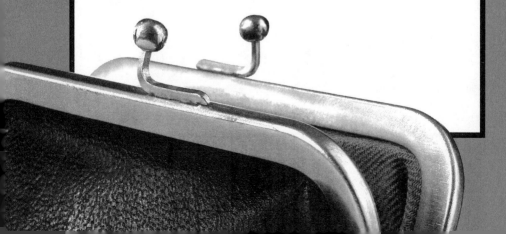

## SELF-ASSESSMENT: WHAT ARE YOUR THOUGHTS ON TALKING ABOUT MONEY?

- ☐ I don't like to talk about money.
- ☐ I don't bring it up unless the client asks.
- ☐ I always feel nervous saying what I charge.
- ☐ When the client asks for a price, I feel I have to answer immediately.
- ☐ If I ask a client's budget and they don't tell me, I drop the subject right away.
- ☐ I blurt out numbers without thinking it through.
- ☐ When the scope of a project changes, I don't know how to tell the client, so I don't.
- ☐ I can't afford to say no to a project.
- ☐ I often put off the money discussion until it's too late.
- ☐ I think it's time to get serious about talking about money.

No matter how many boxes you checked above, you are not alone. Whether quoting a price or asking for payment, many of your colleagues struggle with similar issues, even if they've been in business a while. But the fact is, life is so much better when these "issues" don't get in the way. You can continue living this way or commit to developing the skills and refining the language to ask for what you want. You decide.

# CHAPTER 6
# FINDING AND QUALIFYING YOUR PROSPECTS

"Bigger clients are usually better clients. Big doesn't automatically mean larger budgets and easier to work with, but there is a strong correlation. Also, the farther removed a contact is from the direct impact of a project's cost, the more pricing flexibility and less hassle that can be expected."

—CAMERON FOOTE, EDITOR OF
THE CREATIVE BUSINESS NEWSLETTER

So many creative professionals seem to believe that the problem with their pricing is them, either that their prices are too high or they aren't good enough at selling. One creative said, "I don't know how to turn prospects into customers. I need to learn how to close clients better."

That may be so, but sometimes, you are not the problem. They—the clients—are.

If you're not talking to the right people in the first place, it doesn't matter how you "close" or what you say; the price won't be right because they can't afford your services.

In other words, many pricing problems—when they can't pay what you charge—have a marketing solution. If you haven't qualified your prospects to make sure you're talking to the right people, all the techniques you learn here won't work.

How do you ascertain if these people can, or are willing to, pay? How do you find the ones who will?

Good old-fashioned shoe leather, real or virtual. For example, if you've chosen healthcare technology as a target market, find a place online where you can get your questions answered by industry leaders. Start by joining a few industry groups on LinkedIn.com. If you don't see a discussion related to your services, start your own. Here is one approach:

> "I am researching this industry as a potential market for my (design/copywriting/etc) business. I have a few questions. Any feedback would be much appreciated. Here's what I'd like to know:
>
> • Does this industry value creative services and are you willing to pay for them?
> • Do you hire (fill in the blank) services? If so, for what types of projects?
> • Who should I be reaching out to? Marketing Directors? CEOs? Who else?"

The most effective offline strategy is to get in a room with some living, breathing prospects in your target market so you can make a personal appeal for information. Here are a couple more questions to add that are more appropriate one-on-one:

> "At what point in the process do you start thinking about these services?"
>
> "If we were to offer this service, would you be willing to pay $X?"

## WHEN YOU THINK THEY NEED YOUR HELP...

You may think a prospect needs your help, but do *they* think so? If a company with a hideous-looking or poorly written website doesn't realize it—and don't forget, it is all subjective—or the company doesn't believe it is important enough to improve, don't waste your marketing time trying to persuade them. Instead spend that time finding prospects who are aware of what they need and can pay for it.

### LOOKING FOR YOUR IDEAL CLIENT

Picture your best client. What do they need from you? How often do they need you? What kind of projects do they have?

That data is gold. It's worth the time to analyze your best clients instead of chasing prospects with good intentions but little real potential. Keep handy a running list of characteristics against which you can measure potential clients. Some of these will be universal; others specific to you and your business.

In the end, however, most creative professionals are looking for the same thing in their ideal client: an organization that needs the services you are best suited to provide and pays fairly and on time for them; and a contact who respects your skills, values your services and doesn't drive you crazy.

Who wouldn't want that? But does simply having this dream description help you find these people? Do you recognize them when you see them across a crowded room? Or are your ideal clients slipping through your fingers because you haven't yet identified them clearly enough?

The difference between your Ideal and your Typical Client may be subtle, but it's important. It could be as simple as a company with a monthly project versus a one-off project. Or it could be the fact that they don't have someone on staff who does what you do. Or that they get easily overwhelmed and need someone to turn to in a pinch. Listen for these issues when you are talking with your client. If you can recognize them when they come along, you will be ready to respond and jump into action.

Think about every aspect of the best client you ever had and how they're different from your typical client. Then use that list to identify others just like them, essentially cloning them. Conrad Winter, the Backpocket Copywriter, came up with this short list based on his best client:

- New Jersey-based agency with one office and up to ten employees
- Vertical industry focus in following areas: liquor/beer, real estate, higher education, consumer electronics, retail
- No copywriter on staff
- They value copywriting services (he could tell by looking at their websites and other materials)

Be sure to qualify your prospects for compatibility as well. This isn't about only working with people you "like," but it helps if you and your client can be honest with, and respectful of, each other. You want to make the experience as pleasant and stress-free as possible.

Now it's your turn to define your ideal client.

# CAN YOU PICK YOUR IDEAL CLIENTS OUT OF A LINEUP?

This worksheet will help you discover what separates your Typical Clients from your Ideal Clients—the ones you can help the best—so you can find them and pursue them.

What do they say when they know they need your services and are ready to move forward? That's what you should be listening for—and it takes good listening skills to discern. To determine what your Typical Clients and your Ideal Clients say, fill in the blanks for this blurb by using the checklists below. Select as many items from each column that apply.

## PART 1: YOUR TYPICAL CLIENT

This is what your Typical Client would say to you: "Our _____
                                                       TYPE OF BUSINESS
is in the _____ and we offer _____.
          THEIR INDUSTRY                      WHAT THEY OFFER
We have approximately_____ with an estimated annual
                        NUMBER OF EMPLOYEES
revenue of _____ and we do business _____.
            ANNUAL REVENUE                            LOCATION
What we'd like from you is _____and we
                                    WHAT THEY NEED
need it _____ and we are willing to pay _____.
         HOW OFTEN                                      THEIR BUDGET
Your services are _____ to us."
                  ESSENTIAL/A LUXURY

| TYPE OF BUSINESS | THEIR INDUSTRY | WHAT THEY OFFER |
|---|---|---|
| ☐ for-profit | ☐ finance | ☐ services |
| ☐ nonprofit | ☐ healthcare | ☐ products |
| ☐ large corporation | ☐ technology | ☐ retail |
| ☐ small business | ☐ publishing | ☐ online |
| ☐ solopreneur | ☐ government | ☐ business to business |
| ☐ other_____ | ☐ other_____ | ☐ other_____ |

| NO. OF EMPLOYEES | ANNUAL REVENUE | LOCATION |
|---|---|---|
| ☐ 0–10 | ☐ 10K to 50K | ☐ local |
| ☐ up to 50 | ☐ 50K to 100K | ☐ regional |
| ☐ up to 100 | ☐ up to 500K | ☐ U.S. only |
| ☐ more than 100 | ☐ millions | ☐ U.S. and international |
| ☐ thousands | ☐ billions | ☐ international only |
| ☐ other_____ | ☐ other_____ | ☐ other_____ |
| **WHAT THEY NEED** | **HOW OFTEN** | **THEIR BUDGET** |
| ☐ routine maintenance | ☐ daily | ☐ high |
| ☐ annual project | ☐ weekly | ☐ average |
| ☐ ongoing projects | ☐ monthly | ☐ low |
| ☐ multiple projects | ☐ once in a while | ☐ cheap |
| ☐ one-off projects | ☐ rarely | ☐ obscene |
| ☐ other_____ | ☐ other_____ | ☐ other_____ |

Once you've filled in the blanks, read the blurb out loud. This will give you the language you are likely to hear from your Typical Clients. Move on to Part 2 of this worksheet to see how the language of your Ideal Client differs from that of your Typical Client.

## PART 2: YOUR IDEAL CLIENT

Use the same lists of choices to create the language you want to hear from your Ideal Clients. Select as many items from each column that apply.

This is what your Ideal Client would say to you: "Our _____
<small>TYPE OF BUSINESS</small>
is in the _____ and we offer _____.
<small>THEIR INDUSTRY</small>　　　　　　　　　　<small>WHAT THEY OFFER</small>
We have approximately _____ with an estimated annual
<small>NUMBER OF EMPLOYEES</small>
revenue of _____ and we do business _____.
<small>ANNUAL REVENUE</small>　　　　　　　　　<small>LOCATION</small>
What we'd like from you is _____ and we
<small>WHAT THEY NEED</small>

need it _____ and we are willing to pay _____.
HOW OFTEN                                    THEIR BUDGET
Your services are _____ to us."
ESSENTIAL/A LUXURY

| TYPE OF BUSINESS | THEIR INDUSTRY | WHAT THEY OFFER |
|---|---|---|
| ☐ for-profit | ☐ finance | ☐ services |
| ☐ nonprofit | ☐ healthcare | ☐ products |
| ☐ corporation | ☐ technology | ☐ retail |
| ☐ small business | ☐ publishing | ☐ online |
| ☐ solopreneurs | ☐ government | ☐ business to business |
| ☐ other_____ | ☐ other_____ | ☐ other_____ |

| NO. OF EMPLOYEES | ANNUAL REVENUE | LOCATION |
|---|---|---|
| ☐ 0–10 | ☐ 10K to 50K | ☐ local |
| ☐ up to 50 | ☐ 50K to 100K | ☐ regional |
| ☐ up to 100 | ☐ up to 500K | ☐ U.S. only |
| ☐ more than 100 | ☐ millions | ☐ U.S. and international |
| ☐ thousands | ☐ billions | ☐ international only |
| ☐ other_____ | ☐ other_____ | ☐ other_____ |

| WHAT THEY NEED | HOW OFTEN | THEIR BUDGET |
|---|---|---|
| ☐ routine maintenance | ☐ daily | ☐ high |
| ☐ annual project | ☐ weekly | ☐ average |
| ☐ ongoing projects | ☐ monthly | ☐ low |
| ☐ multiple projects | ☐ once in a while | ☐ cheap |
| ☐ one-off projects | ☐ rarely | ☐ obscene |
| ☐ other_____ | ☐ other_____ | ☐ other_____ |

Once you've filled in the blanks, read this blurb out loud. This is what your Ideal Clients will say. Compare the two blurbs so you'll know the subtle differences to listen for.

## Weeding Out the "Bad"

Difficult clients are on the opposite end of the spectrum from Ideal Clients but you need an equally well-tuned sensitivity to quickly recognize them too. That's essentially what the qualifying process is for.

Look for:

- **Respect.** How do they treat you? Like an employee or a partner? Do they show respect for your work and your process? Do they expect you to drop everything and focus on them? If so, is it because they have an urgent need and are willing to pay the price to get it done? Or does this seem to be their way of doing business? Do they realize you have other clients and projects and you will have to fit them in?

- **Trust.** Will they be micromanaging the project with you as the lackey, or are they coming to you for your expertise? Will they put their trust in you or question you every step of the way?

- **Substance.** Do they seem to know what they're doing? Or do you sense they're going nowhere fast? Are you confident that they have the resources to pay your fees and can execute your great ideas?

- **Fairness.** Are they willing to pay for what they need? Or are they trying to get as much as possible at the lowest price?

Listen for:

- **Experience.** Have they done this before? You can tell by how they describe what they need and the questions they ask. If they don't know what they need, you will spend more time defining the project and describing your process, which should affect your pricing.

- **How they found you.** Always ask and if they say, "I saw something you did and want you to do something like that for us," they may be pre-sold on you, which will make your job easier. If they found you in a random online search and want you to explain why they should hire you, you've got some work ahead and that should affect your price too.

- **Confidence.** Is their plan realistic and credible? Are they confident they can accomplish their goals? If not, your hard work may all be for naught or you may never get to the end of the project.

- **Order.** Is your contact organized or disorganized? Do they follow through on what they say they'll do or do they consistently let things fall through the cracks? And how many people are involved in the process? Projects with multiple decision-makers, even if they're all nice people, can be disorderly time-wasters. If you decide to accept this type of project, prepare in advance and anticipate the problems. Warn about extra hours involved and figure an extra fee into your proposal. You can also recommend (or even require) that they elect one to be the point-person.

### What to Watch Out For

Keep your eyes open for those pesky red flags we've all ignored: a marketing director being pressured from above who doesn't have time to answer your basic questions, or a creative director who holds out the carrot of more work later if you'll just cut your price in half for this project, or a CEO who refuses to pay a deposit because he's been burned in the past or an editor who speaks condescendingly to you or to a colleague. Pay particular attention if:

- Their first question is, "How much does X cost?"
- They want it yesterday.
- They don't want to pay your rates.
- They want you to clean up someone else's mess.
- They don't answer your questions completely or at all.
- They badmouth other creative professionals. When a new prospect starts bad-mouthing someone you're replacing, you're on notice. Don't hesitate to go find that creative pro and ask what happened.

Determine what red flags are acceptable to you and which ones will drive you crazy. Then choose your clients accordingly. You'll be much happier.

### Calculate the "Aggravation" Factor

Emily Cohen advises watching for warning signals that indicate potential future challenges. Cohen's list includes, but is not limited to, clients who are:

- disorganized
- uneducated about creative services
- not the primary decision-maker
- time consumers (e.g., engaging in long calls or meetings unnecessarily)

• disrespectful of your time (e.g., unwilling to return your calls/e-mails)

In these cases, she suggests adding 25 percent (or more) to your fees as a hidden but important "aggravation tax."

---

## ARE YOU WORKING WITH AMATEUR CLIENTS?

The "amateur" clients complain more, pay less and take more of your time than "professional" clients. To them, creative services are like fast food. They want the fastest and the cheapest. They have done no planning and tend to have unrealistic expectations. They've never worked with someone like you and don't know the cost implications. They are impulsive and disorganized, and their chaos readily infiltrates your interactions. They think they know what they need; your job is to execute what they have in mind. They don't understand that you could provide a fresh, professional approach.

Learn to spot the amateurs a mile away, well before you get involved.

---

### Declining Projects That Aren't a Good Fit

Should you take difficult clients or clients who aren't a good fit for you just because you need the money?

That is a question creative professionals face every day, and only you can answer it for yourself. Experience shows, however, that if you give in, you usually pay the price—in mental anguish and time wasted, time that could be used finding better clients.

Saying yes because you can't say no is a bigger problem. Learning to say no is an essential skill for running a successful business (and for life too). Maybe you don't know how or don't want to hurt anyone's feelings. Maybe you're just a bit too polite.

When a prospect's budget isn't enough, veteran designer Petrula Vrontikis simply says,

💬 "You haven't allocated enough resources for this project."

It's up to the client to increase the budget or find another resource. Here are a couple other phrases to try:

💬 "I don't think we're best suited to help you. Your project doesn't fit into our area of expertise."

"The timing isn't right for us to work on this project. Our workload is close to capacity and I'm afraid we wouldn't do our best work for you."

"My minimum project fee is $X. Otherwise, I can't afford to take it on."

You can say these things on the phone, via e-mail or in a letter. The trick is not to overexplain. All you owe them is clarity. Whenever possible, refer another resource. If you wouldn't wish the prospect on your enemy, simply decline it and move on.

Instead of being hurt or offended, the prospect may in fact be grateful. They might even respect you for it, especially if you give them resources that are more suited to their needs.

📖 For more about qualifying clients, read *Stop Pushing Me Around: A Workplace Guide for the Timid, Shy and Less Assertive*, by Ilise Benun, Career Press, 2006.

# CHAPTER 7
# BROACHING THE TOPIC OF MONEY

"Don't expect to be comfortable when telling people what you charge. Stretch yourself. If you stay in your comfort zone, you won't make that much money. Be uncomfortable. Eventually, the stretch will feel normal. When it does, stretch yourself again."

**—MIKELANN VALTERRA, CERTIFIED FINANCIAL RECOVERY COACH AND AUTHOR**

A conversation with a new prospect usually begins very positively. They're interested in your work and you are eager to learn about their project. You ask a lot of questions about the organization, the challenges of their marketplace—all important information. The more you talk, the stronger the bond you forge, the better your chances of a successful project. None of this can happen without the back and forth of conversation.

Eventually money will come up. Will you bring it up or will they? Will you squirm and stutter? Will you put it off, thinking the time isn't right? (Is it ever?) Will you avoid it completely? Or will you tolerate the discomfort? That's the focus of this chapter.

## ANXIOUS ABOUT TALKING MONEY?
## YOU'RE NOT ALONE

Lots of people feel awkward talking about money—socially, professionally, personally. In some countries, talking about money is considered gauche or tacky; entire negotiations are handled without ever directly talking money. In the United States, a society rooted in capitalism and fixated on quantity, talking about money is strangely taboo.

For creative professionals, many of whom are ambivalent about money and business in general, the issues go beyond cultural taboos. The "starving artist" mentality pervades much of the creative fields. Fear also seems to run rampant. But fear of what exactly? Fear of being perceived as greedy if you deal with money well or make too much of it? Fear that clients will think your prices are too high and you'll get no work at all? These beliefs and others are often used as obstacles to earning a good living—one that allows you to support yourself and your family with your creative enterprise.

### Clients Have Issues, Too

In Part 1, you spent some time uncovering your own issues about money. But have you ever stopped to wonder how your prospects and clients feel about dealing with money? Do you think it's a breeze for them? Do you assume that those you perceive as high-powered corporate executives with big budgets are 100 percent at ease? They may not be.

The corporate environment, unpredictable as it is, can produce free-floating anxiety. True, when a client is spending a corporate budget rather than his or her own personal money, it may smooth out some wrinkles of negotiation. But a project with a big price tag will expose your clients to what may feel like scrutiny from above. Their budgets are constantly changing (often shrinking) along with the state of the industry and perhaps the economy. Cuts come down, people are laid off, money that was already slotted disappears. Projects that were given the go-ahead—including your proposals—suddenly "aren't happening."

Even if the situation isn't dire, your clients are probably under the gun to deliver more for less. In fact, their mandate to deliver a lot more for a lot less may come from a boss who is clueless about how creative work gets done. Or your client may simply have too much on their plate.

Maybe you're dealing with a business owner anxious about taking a risk on a new resource. Or a junior professional new to the company and worried about selling you up the chain. Or a seasoned executive who is new to the industry and wants to ensure he or she isn't taken advantage of. Your client may be uncomfortable because she doesn't know enough about what she's asking for or because she's out of touch with how much things cost. These are all things you could listen for.

## Do You Need Confidence to Talk Money?

Confidence, or lack thereof, is part of the problem. You may believe you need to have "confidence" before you can achieve x, y or z. Without it, you can't negotiate that big contract with a formidable client, for example. But confidence is not an "object" one possesses.

In fact, things actually work the other way. Confidence is the byproduct of experience. Through trial and error—mostly error—confidence develops. The more you practice the action you're not so confident about, the better you will get, and as with anything, the better you get, the more confident you will feel the next time, learning as you go. Confidence will not develop if you don't try and don't err. That is especially true when it comes to talking about money and pricing.

## WHEN TO TALK ABOUT MONEY

Believe it or not, many creatives get deep into projects without settling on a price, sometimes without broaching the topic of money at all—that's how distressing the topic can be.

Have you ever avoided the topic altogether? You end a call or meeting where it could and should have been discussed but no one brought it up, including you. You were having such a nice time talking about the project that you didn't want to screw it up by bringing up money. Afterwards, you rationalize, telling yourself that "the vibe" didn't feel right to talk about money. Or you say to yourself, "Let's just get a bit further into the project and then we'll bring it up."

But when is the right time? And what exactly is the right vibe for money talk? Maybe there isn't one.

When you buy a car or a house, no one ever says, "Let's not spoil the whole thing by talking price." Right? Why is your business any different? If you have genuine reason to believe the air would suddenly get sucked out of the room because you mention money, that's one big red flag.

## Should You Talk Money Right Away?

Right away or wait? And, if so, how long?

Problem is, there is no rule. It's different for every single situation and there are several points in a normal prospecting and sales process at which it could naturally come up. Here are general guidelines for how to talk about money at each stage:

1. **Initial Contact.** In this preliminary phase with a new prospect, you're deciding whether it's worth your time (and theirs) to build a relationship. Should you start with a phone call or take the time to meet in person? Often it will depend on whether they can afford your services, which you need to know sooner rather than later. To find out, test the waters by floating some general price ranges as you're talking. Do they blink? Stop breathing? Pause uncomfortably? Skip over it as if it's a minor detail?

2. **Proposal?** You got past the initial contact and they seem fine with your general price range but now there is a project on the table and it's time to decide whether to do a proposal. Get more specific about pricing for the project at hand and run it by your prospect verbally (on the phone, not via e-mail) to see if it fits their budget. Get an okay on this before spending hours on a proposal.

3. **Proposal Presentation.** By now, you've discussed the parameters of a project, written your proposal and are

ready to present it. If you haven't already, it's time to get specific and commit to a price.

**4. Handling Objections.** If price is one of the objections your prospect has, now is when the negotiation begins. Your fee is one element but certainly not the only one. (See Chapter 8: Talking Price and Negotiating.)

**5. Closing the Sale.** Here is when you close the negotiation and either come to terms or not. You must know your bottom line in order to close the sale.

## How to Respond to "What's the Price for a [Fill in the Blank]?"

Here's a typical situation: Cindy gets an e-mail message out of the blue from a small business owner who found her online and wants a price for a website. Cindy's excited to get inquiries "from" her website. She doesn't quite trust herself to say the right thing when she really wants the job and doesn't want to jeopardize the opportunity. So she responds via e-mail, giving her prospect what she's asking for: a price.

That is the easiest thing to do—and potentially the most dangerous from a business development point of view.

It's easy because all Cindy has to do is reply with a number, but it's dangerous because when you send prices to a stranger without having any conversation, without positioning or context or project details, you give over control and essentially say, "I'm not that interested." This can cost you the job.

Prospects who ask first about price raise a red flag. What could it mean? That the prospect's main criterion is price not value? That they've been burned? That they're cheap? You won't know until you talk to them.

If Cindy really wants the project, she will pick up the phone—a phone call in response to an e-mail inquiry speaks volumes about your level of interest—or respond with a message asking to schedule a call. This puts Cindy in the driver's seat and is the first step toward the positioning discussed in Chapter 5: Positioning Your Price.

## HOW MUCH IS A LOGO?

I often get new people who ask, "How much is a logo?" One day I said, "Well, I don't know—how much is a car?" Big pause—then the caller started laughing. But he got the point, and we were able to create a range. If the prospect had been a real estate agent, I would have asked, "How much is a house?"

When a client is really dithering, I roll out the Floor/Ceiling analogy. I say, "Here's the deal: you have a budget ceiling over which you can't go, and I have a floor under which I can't get your work done. If your ceiling is under my floor, we will need to figure out how we can tailor your project to get it between the two." This usually gets the conversation back on track, unless their ceiling is not realistic and they won't budge (which is a clear sign that they are not my client). It also helps to lighten up the conversation.

Laurel Black is owner of Laurel Black Design.

### How to Respond to "What Is Your Hourly Rate?"

Creatives get this question all the time and often give the easy answer: a number, unadorned. $50 or $150 or $300—the number itself is irrelevant. What's relevant is that it requires no conversation.

It can be tempting to answer this way, even a force of habit, especially if you don't like talking money. But, as was established in Chapter 3: Setting Your Prices, when it comes to something as subjective as creative services, talking about hourly rates (or any other quantifiable unit of measure) diminishes the perceived value of your talents, cheapens the enterprise and turns it into a commodity that your prospect can get for less (often much less on the Internet).

If you respond to the question with your hourly rate, they may start immediately comparing you to other creative professionals, despite stark qualitative differences, essentially comparing apples to oranges. Or they may stop listening to the carefully constructed explanation of your creative process and start calculating what they think it should cost or, worse, how much you earn, perhaps compared to what they earn. Don't let them go there.

Unless you're talking about on-site freelancing, which is commonly paid hourly, it will serve you best to respond to this question by proposing a project fee as an alternative and framing it as "good news" for them, which it actually is. Here are a few variations to try:

> "I don't charge per hour because it's not good for my clients. What's far more helpful to you is to know what this is going to cost. We'll agree on a scope of work and a fee for it and you'll know what you've got."

> "We quote by the project, not by the hour, and I'm going to come up with my best estimate and I will give you a number, a fixed fee,

so you don't have to worry that once things get under way, I'll throw up my hands and say, 'Sorry, but now the meter is running.'"

"I don't bill my time that way. It's far better, for me but especially for you, to give you a fixed fee. It's all too easy for a simple project to turn into more hours because the meter always feels like it's running. That way, you don't go into a project wondering how many hours are going by. Instead, you know this job is going to cost $X with these stipulations. You have a clear line item in your budget, barring some unforeseen addition of work or scope creep."

## What Do They Really Want to Know?

Sometimes, when a prospect asks first for a price or your hourly rate, that's not necessarily what they want or need to know at that moment. To find out what is, you must listen for the question underneath. Do they want to know how you bill? Are they asking about your process? The amateur clients especially may be unfamiliar with the way creative services work; others are trying to get a sense of where you fit in the world of creatives.

User experience design consultant Mona Patel believes, "It's not smart to discuss actual prices too soon, because once you do, you're both stuck with the numbers you've put on the table. The longer you wait, the more information you gather, the more accurate your price will be. By talking about the project and its scope without mentioning price, you are essentially buying yourself more freedom in the pricing. If you name your price too soon, it will be harder to negotiate down, even if you want to."

Listen to an interview on when to discuss price at www.creative freelancerblog.com /money-guide.

If you take the lead, you can engage your prospect in a different conversation. In fact, be like a politician: don't accept the premise of the question. Instead, direct the conversation where you think it needs to go before you talk about price—essentially positioning your price before you give it.

Mona recommends this response to buy you time:

> "I would be happy to provide a competitive price; however, I can only develop that once I understand your requirements better. May I ask you more questions?"

This way, you successfully drive the conversation to the more relevant topic of value: "What is this project worth to you?" This is more appropriate because it leads to more open communication, clarity and a stronger relationship, which is worth the potentially uncomfortable exchange it takes to get there.

# CHAPTER 8
# TALKING PRICE AND NEGOTIATING

"Money is too important to be left to paper alone (or, heaven forbid, e-mail)."

—CAMERON FOOTE, EDITOR OF THE
CREATIVE BUSINESS NEWSLETTER

With the most promising prospects, a moment will come—ideally before you write the proposal—when you will talk about actual numbers. You should have a strong indication that the project, client and budget are a good fit before you put pen to paper. Many creative professionals skip this step completely, instead going directly to writing a full-length proposal.

If you skip the initial money discussion, there may be a price to pay: time wasted on proposals you lose because your price was too high and because you didn't bring it up earlier.

## LET'S TALK ABOUT MONEY

There are many ways to segue to the money conversation. Most are variations on the simple theme of, "Let's talk about money." Experiment with the various approaches below to see what works best for you.

1. Be matter of fact.

💬 "We've talked about everything else. Now, let's talk about the cost."

Note the use of "the cost" and not "our fees." This is about what it costs to do what they need done, not what "you" will charge. Precise language makes it more objective and professional.

2. Take the pressure off.

💬 "It's helpful to get the money thing rolling. We don't have to settle it this minute, but I wanted to give you some ideas about what we should be thinking."

Note the use of "we" to imply that this is an agreement you came to together.

3. Give them your thinking.

💬 "Here's how we think about the money."

This approach implies you've given it thought and you've done this a lot, instilling confidence and credibility.

4. Make a joke.

💬 "Here's everyone's favorite part of the conversation."

Making light of it acknowledges any potential awkwardness on their part as well as yours.

## Gauging the Budget

Always, always, always begin the money conversation by asking for their budget. This may be obvious, but many creatives neglect to ask this basic question.

There are many ways to ask:

💬 "What is your budget?"

"What do you have in mind to spend?"

"What can you afford?"

"What budget have you allocated for this project?" (The construction of this question presumes they have allocated a budget.)

In the best-case scenario, your prospect will simply tell you the budget. Often they won't. But remember, this is a discussion, not a confrontation. You need this information to determine if writing a proposal is worth the time. So don't give up so easily. Probe, using your creativity, to reveal information that will help you decide. But what exactly to say?

Experiment with this. First, suggest a fairly wide range:

💬 "Are we talking $5,000 or $25,000?"

You may fear that they'll automatically choose your lowest number but at this point you're not quoting a price. You're just trying to gauge budget. Most good prospects won't choose the lowest number because that usually indicates low quality. If they affirm the low number, that may be your cue to walk away. You can also try giving three options to choose from.

💬 "Is it as low as $5,000, as much as $15,000, or as high as $25,000?"

When presented with three choices, they may lean toward the one in the middle.

### "We Don't Have A Budget"

When the client says this, it could have any number of meanings, although it rarely means the sky's the limit. It could mean...

**I don't have much to spend.** This should be treated like a red flag. They can't expect you to do it for nothing, but with a very limited budget, this prospect could be buying on price only. If you're looking for a straight fee for your services, this may be a good time to refer the project to someone else. However, if there are other things you would value from this prospect—such as visibility or connections to other prospects—you may enter into a negotiation about it.

**I don't know what this should cost.** Some clients really won't know. They're new to the job or the industry or the medium or to working with creatives. If they really don't know, you can inform them. But that doesn't necessarily mean they have no number in mind. In fact, sometimes, they will claim not to know, so you give them your price and they respond with, "Oh no, that's outside my budget." Aha! They did have a budget! They're not liars. It's just that they may not have been aware of the number in their mind. You've helped them reveal it.

By the way, just because they don't have a "budget" doesn't mean you can't find out what they are thinking of spending. Keep probing. You can say: "There are many ways to approach this and I will pull together a formal quote. But normally, for this type of work the range is from $X to $Y. How does that sit?"

It can be risky to be this specific if you haven't collected the requirements for the job. But if you are confident about the pricing, try it. Just be careful what numbers you float, especially in a real-time conversation. If you're not sure, buy yourself some time to think about it before continuing the conversation.

**I don't want to share my budget.** This is the most common meaning of "We don't have a budget." This is essentially, "Just tell me what it costs." They may say this in a way that is abrasive, but don't be intimidated. The point is to keep the conversation going, to make sure you're in the same ballpark.

Some prospects may not be willing to "cough up" numbers, and you risk annoying them if you push too far. But it's worth pushing a bit. Be sensitive, but not paranoid.

You can try:

> "Our services can be infinitely tailored to meet your specific needs. So if you tell me what number you have in mind, I'll tell you what you can get for that."

Jennifer Neal of K9 Design Co. explains it to her clients this way, "I could give you the best quote in the world, but if it's higher than your budget, it wouldn't matter. So that's why it would help to know your budget."

Kit Hinrichs of Studio Hinrichs cuts to the chase: "Look, we can dance around each other about this, but we're trying to find the best way to spend your money effectively. So if we know what budget you have in mind, we can find solutions for you that are within your budget."

Andy Strote of Context Creative suggests trying, "If you had a marketing budget, what would it be?" He'll try five different ways until he gets an answer.

Writer Doug Dolan probes diplomatically. "If you can't share your budget, I respect that and I will go away and come back to you with a quote based on my best estimate of what I think it will take. But because there are so many variables, it can be very helpful—it's up to you, of course—if you give me an idea of how much you have to work with. With so many moving parts to this project, there are too many chances for misunderstanding. That's why I'm pushing a bit for a number. Whether I know your budget or not, I've got to give you a convincing breakdown of what I'm proposing."

Keep in mind that, after all your efforts, they still may not tell you the actual budget. But don't let them stop you from probing as much as you sense will be tolerated.

Dana Manciagli, general manager at Microsoft Corporation and a buyer of creative services who will not give a budget when asked, says, "Fewer than 20 percent of clients will give you the budget, but if you don't ask, you won't know. It's a chicken and egg situation. Many clients need to get a quote and then ask their boss for the money. I always like tying it to an assessment of my needs, which flows to a logical quote... like a story unfolding. The story is not about the money, it's about a successful creative outcome with a fair price."

Manciagli believes doing proposals is part of playing the odds game. "If doing full-length proposals takes too long," she suggests, "why not develop a simple template with the project's requirements and some general pricing?"

That's exactly what Mona Patel does. "I do very few full-length proposals that I don't think are going to close. If at all possible, I like to get a verbal close before writing the proposal. I give them a number and they will either say, 'Go ahead and write it up,' or 'That seems high but maybe if I see it written out it will make more sense.' At that point, I will do an executive summary or a one-page recap of what we discussed."

## THE REALITY OF CLIENT BUDGETS

### BY CAMERON FOOTE

Let's start with a common misconception, particularly among those having limited experience inside client organizations. It is that budgets are the result of expert and extensive management deliberation. That is, that the budget for any given project or program is set only after a lengthy review of priorities, finances and market norms. It is, therefore, both a true reflection of what the organization can afford and the prevailing market price.

Actually, this isn't even close to what is typically the case. In reality, most organizations set budgets arbitrarily and more by happenstance than managerial science. This is especially true in areas where the client has little expertise, or where the return (ROI) from the amount budgeted can't be easily measured—the very definition of most creative projects and programs. The smaller the organization, the more this holds true.

A client's budget-setting exercise often consists of guesstimating what someone thinks something should cost. Or it might consist of extrapolating cost figures from a past activity without any regard to inflation or differences. Or it is simply what the client feels is affordable.

This makes you the budget expert—for a reason no more complicated than project pricing is something you do all the time and they do almost never. A price honestly figured by an experienced firm that knows its labor costs, expenses and how long things actually take will always be closer to the market average than what appears in a client's budget.

Another misconception is that client budgets are sort of etched in granite. In reality, the more specific an item is, the less this is so. For example, a corporate marketing department may, indeed, have to keep within its total budget for promotion. But it can overspend lavishly on some projects as long as it cuts back on others. In other cases, a budget might be just a guideline, much the same as individuals might use a household budget to keep expenses more or less in line with income.

Client budgets should be taken as guidelines, seldom literally. Any good client would rather have a proposal focused on the best thing to do rather than simply meeting an arbitrary number. That said, try to prepare a first proposal around the client's best interests, as long as it can fall within 15 percent of their budget. (A higher discrepancy would probably look opportunistic. If their budget is totally out of touch with reality, it is best to talk with them first.)

If, after presentation, the client insists on sticking to the budget, be prepared to present a second proposal that meets it. This approach doesn't ignore the legitimate wishes of clients. It simply recognizes that they shouldn't be expected to predict in advance what approach will work best or how much it will cost. This is why, after all, clients call in outside professionals in the first place.

The takeaway here is that there is nothing sacrosanct about a client's budget figure. It may be realistic, but it is probably more likely not to be. If it turns out to be inadequate, there should be no reluctance to ask that it be increased, or that the project be modified to fit it.

> Inadequate budgets, whether the result of lack of funding or inexperience, are not your problem. It's the client's problem. Your job is to let them know.
>
> Cameron Foote is editor of the *Creative Business* newsletter (www.creativebusiness.com).

### What If You Forget to Broach the Topic?

You meant to, really you did, but you got carried away in the conversation and before you knew it, you hung up or walked out and now it's too late—you've told them you'd send the proposal. It's just too late to go back and ask for their budget.

Or is it? Of course not. Wait an hour or wait a day, whatever you feel you need, but do call back and say:

> "You know what? I've been thinking about your project and I have a few more questions."

Maybe you really just have that one money question you need answered or maybe you have been thinking about the project and you do in fact have more questions and the budget question is one of them.

### Anticipate Scope Creep

Because the nature of the creative process is iterative, it is standard practice to agree to a certain number of revisions; that number is negotiable and should be part of the conversation before the contract is signed.

It's important at this stage to explain your revision process as well. Articulate as well as you can where the line falls between revisions that are included and those that aren't. What exactly is one "revision"? What constitutes a "round of revisions"? What's the difference between major and minor revisions? Is a small change in many places the same as a large change that only affects one aspect of a project? Is a text change the same as a change to design and layout? Does how long a revision takes determine how extensive or expensive it is? Laying this foundation early on is like insurance against problems later.

Always stress that if you see a change request that looks like it's going to alter the scope of the project, or some other fundamental element, you will be proactive and involve the client in the decision-making process. You can say:

> "We want to draw a line so that when we approach it or go beyond it, we will know it. If we address it right away, there's an opportunity to stop and say, 'Because of the CEO's late night e-mail, we had to add four more pages, which affected this and this. That's why the project is not what we anticipated.' Let's talk about what we are going to do about that."

The emphasis is on the "we" and adds the verbal assurance that you're not just waiting for them to slip over the line.

## NEGOTIATING A CONTRACT

You've come a long way. There's a project on the table for a prospect you're confident can afford your services. You've successfully led the conversation to the topic of money and started talking price. That's where negotiation begins—yet another skill that most creative professionals have no training in and thus avoid. That explains why you may not see all of the options available to you; you may think you must either take what's being offered or leave it. But the third and better option is to negotiate.

Negotiation is:

- where the money conversation gets serious. It's when you each ask for what you want and then come to terms—or not.

- a positioning activity; it positions you to be taken seriously. Business services are by nature negotiable. Your clients expect a counteroffer to their contract or proposal. Ducking the negotiation by accepting the first offer may be perceived as unprofessional and speaks volumes about the way you conduct business.

- the way you take care of yourself. Rushing through a negotiation, or worse, holding your nose while it's happening, will not result in the best outcome for yourself. After all, no one will look out for your interests if you don't.

- a trial period. It's your chance to see how this person or company does business. It's a way of working together without actually committing quite yet. It's a clear window into the working relationship with this person and organization.

You've certainly heard it said that a successful negotiation is a "win-win," which means both parties get at least some of what they want. Nobody gets everything they want. The heart of negotiation is compromise, so start by keeping both parties in mind. But don't give in too quickly or give back too much. You are not at anyone's mercy here, even if it may feel that way. Remember, this is your business.

# Q&A ON NEGOTIATING

**Q:** What is negotiation?
**A:** It's the give and take that occurs to arrive at a decision that affects more than one person.

**Q:** What makes a good negotiator?
**A:** The best negotiators are people who listen carefully to what the other person says and who find out the real motivation driving the other person. The longer you listen, the more you'll find out about what's really important to them. It's not always about money. It could be about time, location, rights, exposure, status, primacy.

**Q:** What is the best attitude with which to approach a negotiation?
**A:** Know that the person on the other side of the table is another person, just like you. Don't be intimidated. Find out their role in the company, as it relates to what you're negotiating. Don't make assumptions about their power. They may just be trying to impress their own superiors.

**Q:** Any more tips?
**A:** A little self-deprecating humor never hurts.

Frank Marciano is an attorney based in Hoboken, New Jersey.

## What Do You Want?

Your challenge in each negotiation is to come to the prover-bial table with the clarity to know what you want, the con-

TALKING PRICE AND NEGOTIATING

To listen to an interview on negotiating, go to www.creative freelancerblog.com /money-guide.

fidence to ask for it and the ability to walk away if you don't get close enough to it.

Sometimes, a negotiation is simple and straightforward. They tell you their budget range, you propose a price and you settle somewhere in the middle. Other times, you go back and forth until you arrive at "terms" both sides can be satisfied with. (Don't agree to terms that you aren't satisfied with; you may end up sabotaging the job because of it.)

So what do you want?

Since this is business, the main ingredient here will be money. Forget about what you think they can afford. Start by knowing how much you need to do the job. Before you go into any negotiation, know your top line—what you want to earn—and your bottom line—the minimum you're willing to take.

Make a list of what you want and what you have to offer. This is like a puzzle where each piece can be moved around, taken away or replaced to make up a whole that both parties will eventually live with—or not.

Everything is negotiable. As the lawyer Frank Marciano said, it's not always about money. In fact, you may think money is the main ingredient in any negotiation, but in reality, there are many other elements that may be more important to your prospects, such as quick turnaround. There may be something your prospect can offer you that may be more valuable to you than money, such as access and introductions to VIPs. This can be a good option to keep in mind when negotiating with nonprofits especially. Do they have board members you'd like to meet? Events you'd like to attend for networking purposes? Can you negotiate to have your name listed as a donor? Don't be shy. Ask for what you want and see what you can get.

If you are asked to remove or revise one or more of your terms, always do so in exchange for something else. For example, high-profile corporations may have policies about having their names used in your marketing. But that may be one of the main reasons you're agreeing to do the job, especially if they claim not to have much of a budget. You may be able to negotiate for using the name in a printed piece but not showing their work on your website, or vice versa.

## Preparing for the Negotiation

When it's time to negotiate, whether in person or on the phone, what do you need to have in front of you? A script or a cheat sheet of questions to ask? Do you need to be in a quiet room where you won't be disturbed? Do you need to shut down your e-mail so that you can focus on the person you're talking to? If so, do that.

Once you've got the concrete details straight, turn your attention to your attitude. Muster all your confidence, faking it if necessary. Keep the big picture in view and remind yourself this is not the only gig in the world. Other opportunities will come along.

Aim for the zen-like state of detachment in which you are prepared to walk away if necessary, but you will do your best to come to terms with this prospect. Walking away closes the door, and it may be better to settle for less so that you can develop a relationship, especially with a coveted client.

## Negotiating Beyond the Contract

You breathe a sigh of relief because the hard part is done and now you get to the fun part: the creative work. But the negotiating and communicating doesn't stop once you sign the contract, alas. Inevitably, there will be issues to address, details that arise, changes that require attention and discussions that, if ignored, become quite thorny issues down the road. Don't drop your business mind-set as you begin the creative work.

And watch like a hawk for scope creep, because the revision process can take on a life of its own and become a minefield for misunderstanding that spins out of control. Things are happening quickly. The revisions just keep coming, and there is no hard and fast line between the second revision, which is included, and the third revision, which is not. On paper, it's clear, but in reality it's a moving target. It doesn't seem like there's time to stop and say, "Hey wait, this is going to cost more." But you must.

There is a moment to watch for and not let slip by. A moment when you know you should speak up. Once that moment is gone, things tend to snowball and then it's too late. You know because you've been there. You are about to say something but you get distracted. Or you just can't come up with the right phrasing. If you let the critical moments pass without speaking up, it will be that much more difficult to recoup and recover later. It is your responsibility to continually educate your clients about what is involved in the changes they request and then decide together if it's worth the time.

But when you have planted the seeds in advance, you're well prepared to seize that moment. The key here is to warn the client as you finish the last included round that any revisions beyond this will be seen as an extra round and will be billed as such. In some cases, the mention of additional fees for more changes magically makes the need for them disappear. The client is suddenly satisfied with your work the way it is. Other clients actually need more revisions than they contracted for and are willing to pay for it. For them, embrace the process; you might even make a profit.

All of this requires diplomacy. It takes practice to learn to say these things in a way that isn't offensive but also responds to each particular situation.

# CHAPTER 9
# CONFIDENTLY CLOSING THE SALE

"Being confident, not defensive, is especially important in pricing out a project. Avoiding discussion, apologizing and aggressive justification are all indications of self-doubt. They call into question pricing legitimacy among good clients; among not-so-good ones they lead to negotiation and haggling."

—CAMERON FOOTE, EDITOR OF THE
CREATIVE BUSINESS NEWSLETTER

The dream scenario, of course, is that you present your proposal. Your prospect asks a question or two, which you answer confidently. They don't bat an eye at your price; it's not even mentioned. Then they smile and say, "Where do I sign?"

This is what you hope will happen, and it sometimes does. But more often than not, you send your proposal and then you wait.

That is actually the worst thing you can do. Waiting to hear from them puts you in a bad position emotionally and tactically.

## WHAT YOU CAN DO TO CLOSE THE SALE

The alternative is to know that the ball is in your court, always. That means there's always more you can do toward closing the sale. Try any and all of these techniques.

### Ask More Questions

To keep the conversation going while they're deciding, you need to know their process, especially where this project fits into their big picture. Projects often stall for reasons beyond your contact's control. If that's happening or could happen, it would be helpful for you to know:

- What are their next steps in the process?
- Who else is going to be involved in the decisions?
- Who are they going to show the proposal to?
- Who else are they talking to? You always have the right to ask that. They may not always tell you, but you absolutely should ask.
- What are their internal deadlines?

These questions, which you may have asked early in the process, help to put flesh on the bones of your relationship with your prospects. Without this information, when you call to see if they've decided yet, it looks like all you care about is whether or not they choose you—which may or may not be true. If you know more about their process, you can say,

"I know you have to produce something for a trade show in two weeks, so if we get started by Monday, I can help you make that deadline."

This may not change their mind, but it could nudge them toward a decision.

## Ask for the Business

The heart of "closing the sale" is asking for the business. But creatives often neglect to do this. You may feel it would be too pushy or you assume the client will come to you when they decide. But if you don't ask for the business, you are a lot less likely to get it.

So, how exactly do you do that? With confidence, whether you feel confident or not, try these closing techniques, standard in sales but adapted for creatives:

### 1. Ask if they are ready.

"Have I answered all your questions? Are you ready to make a decision?"

If the answer is no, find out why. What additional questions or issues are in the way? What else do they need to do or know or take care of before they make a decision? Always be gathering information to keep the conversation going.

### 2. Propose the next step.

"Here is the next step. I will call you on Tuesday to review final details and answer any questions you may have. Is the morning good for you?"

If they're not ready for the next step, they'll make it clear.

**3. Make the next step easy to take.** In other words, create a bridge to cross in order to go from "We're just in the talking stage" to "Now we are working together." You can say something as simple as,

💬 "I'm going to send you our contract to sign. And as soon as we have that, we can get to work."

**4. Get an advance.** Asking for a deposit is another good "next step" and should be a standard part of the process. With small businesses, this should be standard operating procedure, especially with new clients you've never worked with. But with large corporations, quick deadlines may not allow you to wait until you actually receive a check to get started. You can still initiate the process of collecting advance money.

**5. Ask questions they can answer positively.** This keeps them in control and keeps the ball rolling.

💬 "What's the best way to get the contract done?"

"How much time do you need?"

"Who else needs to see it?"

"The sooner the better, right?"

"So would it make sense to send the invoice with that?"

"Should it be flagged in a particular way—to your attention and copied to someone in accounting?"

**6. Give a deadline.**

💬 "I can honor this price structure (or this proposal) until the end of this month."

Or,

💬 "We only have one slot left in our project calendar this month and
⋮ I'd be happy to hold it for you if you decide by Friday."

You can say this whether or not it is the whole truth. It's not a question of deception as much as incentive. The culture has conditioned us to buy within a deadline or with an incentive. We are all subject to that aspect of the culture, including your clients.

Giving them a deadline can be very helpful because it could provide more information. They may say, "Oh, we won't know by then. Or, we can't decide by then." You can ask why not, or extend your deadline or be flexible with it. But at least you'll have a time frame to work against, as opposed to being out there in limbo, not knowing. That's what makes this process anxiety-producing.

If any of these techniques feel too pushy, use a disclaimer like,

💬 "I hope this won't come across as pushy, but I would like to tell you
⋮ what the next step in our process is in case you're ready to take it."

You deflect what you imagine by addressing it directly and verbally. There is no right way to do any of this. That's why it's important to experiment with these techniques.

## WHAT TO DO WHEN YOU'RE NOT SURE IF IT'S A GO

In the real world, the line between scoping out the project and getting started on phase one is not always clear. Sometimes you can't tell whether the project is a go. You're being invited to meetings and you've even started the work, against your better judgment. But the money conversation never got resolved, and needless to say, you have not yet been paid anything.

You may have pitched and proposed a price they agreed to. But as you continue to clarify and broaden the scope of the work, there may be open questions regarding outside resources, which will definitely add to the price. After pinning down the scope of work, you have to go back to price.

You can say,

> "We still haven't made a decision about hiring a photographer. We should start nailing that down. It will help us in the creative process."

Leaving too many of those things unresolved too far into the process can shake your confidence and make you feel like the project is going to get taken away.

Some clients don't discourage that impression. Some do it unconsciously; they make the proving period longer than is reasonable or necessary because they don't want to be exposed or taken advantage of. You're still feeling like you don't want to upset the apple cart with a price and you're already well into the project. Others will deliberately try to make you feel like the job is still hanging in the balance. This is usually a power play and a red flag. These are clients to avoid.

## What to Do While You're Waiting for a Decision

You've come this far. You've asked for the business and they haven't made a decision yet. What do you do, how long should you wait and how often should you follow up?

Of course there is no formula for this either. Each situation is different. But the details you've gathered to date about your prospect, their project and their process should tell you when and how often you should follow up. If it doesn't, you can ask them. Say:

💬 "If you are not ready to make a decision today, would you be ready to talk more next week?"

Which is not to say things won't drag on. They're not on your timetable, after all. They have their own schedule, and it has nothing to do with you. Don't forget that. And if you really want the project—perhaps because it is going to help you get to your goal—be more proactive. Here's how:

**1. Demonstrate that you're thinking about the project by sending ideas that pop into your head.** This can also feel a bit presumptuous, because you're not yet working with them. You can say,

💬 "As I was driving the other day and thinking about the goal you'd like to reach, I had an idea for how to approach the project."

Or,

💬 "I was reading the *Wall Street Journal* and came across this article that reaffirms the hunch you had about the healthcare industry."

Or refer to something that ties up a loose thread from your pitch meeting:

💬 "I was thinking a bit more about what you asked regarding X, and it seems like a good way around that would be to Y…"

Or,

💬 "I talked to one of our web producers and he suggested…"

Don't confuse this with "spec work"—you are not sending comps or sketches or concepts. You're just teasing a bit by sharing your ideas.

**2. Demonstrate your eagerness to learn.** Prospects are often averse to taking risks with new vendors. But they can't help but respond positively to someone who takes initiative and shows curiosity. In fact, if this is a big project that is important to you, it's a good idea to do some research on their industry and competition. They may not be keeping as close an eye on it as they should be.

**3. Set up a "Google Alert" on one or two of their competitors or on their company and pass along what you find.** A Google alert—like a clipping service for the web—will send you links based on selected keywords. So, for instance, you could have a Google alert on your prospect's name or company or competitors or all of the above. Anytime those keywords or keyword phrases are posted on the web or mentioned in a blog post, you'll receive the links via e-mail. It is a really simple way to stay abreast of what is happening and pass that information along. Even if they've already seen it, it shows that you're thinking of them.

**4. Show your professionalism.** Before you start a job, your clients don't have much to judge the quality of your creativity, but they can certainly judge your customer service. So if you can demonstrate that you are responsive, that you are professional, organized and reliable, this could tip the scales in your favor—even if your price is a little higher.

Engagement on the part of their vendors is often what clients are looking for. Don't worry about giving too much information away. Be clear about the distinction between sharing your ideas and the more serious endeavor of turning those ideas into the actual work product. Show them that you're thinking about the project because you are interested and ready to get started when they are. These are all closing techniques.

## UH-OH: THE BLACK HOLE

At a certain point in your follow up, you may stop hearing from your prospect. They won't say, "Sorry, we didn't choose you." You just never hear back. This happens more often than anyone would like to admit. Let's call it the Black Hole.

It happens because they are bombarded from right and left, too many e-mail messages and things on the to-do list and people to respond to and voice mails to listen to and bosses pressuring these poor marketing managers who are, underneath it all, good, decent people. Nice people, who don't have or don't take the time to do what used to be common courtesy, to say, "Here's what happened. We didn't choose you or we decided not to do it." Or whatever!

Instead, they say nothing, and in this black hole you rev up your imagination. And for some reason you start imagining negative things—that's why it's a black hole—that you have no way of knowing about. The project may have been put on hold or the person in charge quit or got laid off and the project dissolved, or any number of things could have happened. But the point is, you don't know, so you shouldn't guess.

You don't know. And you may not ever know. But if you need to ease your own mind, try to find out what happened:

**1. Leave a "final" message.** If you've left several voice and e-mail messages—and you should do both—and you still haven't heard anything, then leave a "final message," which says,

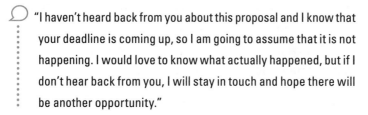

> "I haven't heard back from you about this proposal and I know that your deadline is coming up, so I am going to assume that it is not happening. I would love to know what actually happened, but if I don't hear back from you, I will stay in touch and hope there will be another opportunity."

That way they know that you've closed the book on it, which may trigger them to respond because they don't want you to think the wrong thing. If not, at least you've tied up the loose ends in a professional way, which will be remembered, even if you never know it.

**2. Check in at the mid-point.** Whether or not they chose another creative professional, keep the lines of communication open and check in at the middle of the process to see how it's going. They may be unhappy with the choice they made and grateful to you for following up. Do it in a gracious way; as a "check in" to see how they're doing:

> "I hope it's going well. If there is anything that I can do to help, I am here and I am available."

Friendly, professional and open—that is the message that you want to convey over and over again.

**3. Stay in touch.** Don't disappear into the black hole yourself. Don't assume, "If they are not calling me, they must not want me"—you know how that goes. It can get really ugly inside your own head. Avoid that by staying in touch with your prospect in the real world, whether on Facebook or with a quarterly phone call, with your monthly e-mail newsletter or by following them on Twitter. Whatever tools you use, stay visible and in communication.

### When They Choose Someone Else

Any of these techniques may trigger the response, "We chose someone else." This is actually good, not because they chose someone else, obviously, but because they let you know the decision they made. Don't sulk away. Spring into action, gathering more information, whether about the prospect or about your process and how you can improve it, or about the competition (because whomever they chose is your competition).

You could say,

> "Thank you so much for letting me know. May I ask who you chose and why?"

Notice that you're not asking, "Why didn't you choose us?" You're asking,

> "What was the process you went through? What criteria were important to you? And why did you make the choice that you did?"

It's all about them and not so much about you. Whatever details you can gather will help you do a better job marketing next time, either to them or someone just like them.

By the way, your "competition" may not be who you think it is. In fact, it is whomever you're bidding against. They may not be the type of company or the type of service that you would even consider your competition, but they are because your prospect considers them an option. That's what you need to know: who your prospect considers your competition.

If they do name names, don't ever knock their choice and imply doubt about it. If it's one of your credible competitors, say something like,

💬 "They're a good choice. I hope you do something good together."

That shows a bit of class while introducing a tiny seed of doubt. You didn't say, "I know they'll do a good job for you."

If the firm they chose is an unknown quantity, you can say,

💬 "Oh—I'm afraid I don't know them. I hope it works out well."

If they feel you're plugged in, it will register that they may have gone too far downmarket—again, not enough to reverse their decision, but maybe enough to have them think twice next time.

### "We'll Keep You on File"

Sometimes at this point in the process or even much earlier, when you're just reaching out to new prospects and there is no project even on the table, they will say, "We'll keep you on file." Do they really mean it, or is it just their way of getting rid of you?

How should you respond? Thank them and hang up? No, there is more you can do. Ideally, "on file" means "We're going to put these papers you sent into a file cabinet for future reference." But in our electronic society, there isn't much "paper" to send or keep "on file," so these days it means, "on my computer somewhere."

No matter how organized they are, it's likely they've got a lot of information to keep track of. So when they offer to "keep you on file," take them seriously and say,

> "I'd love to help you keep me on file so if I stay in touch with you by e-mail, would that help you remember that I am here?"

Or, you can ask,

> "I want to help you remember that I am here, so what would be the best way to do that? You tell me what you want."

You're soliciting their preferences, which you should keep track of in a contact management system. That way, you can do what they are asking you to do, which will help you feel more confident about each prospect without feeling pushy.

### When Nothing Seems to Work

Whether you get the project or not, getting this far is an accomplishment. Through the proposal process, you have essentially had the opportunity to engage in a substantial conversation with a promising prospect. They've had a chance to see how you work and—whatever the reason they didn't choose you—you have built a very strong foundation that you should continue to build on. Even if you don't win the project, you have no idea what is coming down the pike later on from this organization.

If your contact moves to another department or a different company, as long as you have made a strong and professional impression and especially if you stay in touch—through e-mail updates and LinkedIn for example—the seeds you planted will have a chance to bloom in the future.

# CHAPTER 10
# GETTING PAID

"I've never seen anyone point you toward the door for having the effrontery to mention money."

**—DOUG DOLAN, WRITER**

You've made it through both the initial money conversation and the negotiation, but there's still some work to do. You still have to get paid and that isn't always smooth, especially if you don't have a process in place for it. Some creative professionals would rather wait for payment than come out and ask for it. Before we get to money management, here's a bit more nitty gritty about how to say what's necessary to get that money in hand.

## SENDING THE FIRST INVOICE: TELL, DON'T ASK

There can be some awkwardness when it's time to send the first invoice. You've discussed terms of payment during the negotiation, but getting that first check can take some doing.

It's not wise to let any self-doubt bleed into comments that make it sound like they have complete control over how things are going to go.

So don't say, "We'd like to send the first invoice if that's okay." Those three extra words are unnecessary and they imply that the client has the sole right to decide whether they're going to pay you or not.

Instead, make it matter of fact:

💬 "We'll send over the first invoice today."

Better yet, use a standard e-mail message to kick off the project. Couch that first request for payment in a context where you revisit what's exciting about the project (especially if you're pushing the envelope on price) and ask a few practical questions, such as where the source material is coming from or who the additional contacts are. It's appropriate to close with, "We'll be sending along the first invoice tomorrow."

The first invoice will usually be for your advance or deposit on the job and should accompany the contract so they can return both at the same time. Make it clear that as soon as you get the paperwork back, you'll get started on the project. You don't have to be rigid about it. And if you're working with a large corporation with a lot of red tape, use your judgment on how much to do before you get a check in hand. Getting started with the work is fine but don't deliver any materials before you see green. You want to show that you trust your client; but being professional means upholding policies, yours as well as theirs. Good clients will respect you for it.

With small businesses—new clients especially—be firmer about your policies and wait for your advance before you start any work. Consider offering credit card payment as an option to facilitate the process for them and get what you need at the same time. If you do this, include a section in your contract stating that if they are delinquent on their bill, they give permission to charge their credit card after a certain number of late days.

## SENDING THE FINAL INVOICE: DON'T WAIT TOO LONG

Getting paid at the end of a project often takes longer than it should too, unless you have some systems in place. You don't always have to wait until there's nothing left to do before you send the final invoice, especially if they've acknowledged how long it takes to get paid. Do, however, get their agreement first.

You can say,

> "We're winding down and here's what's left to do: [list of items left to do]. I'd like to get the final invoice into your system. Does that work on your end?"

This is positioned as a question about their budget or accounting process, not about who's in control of the money. You're asking how it will affect their cash flow or their accounts payable to put the payment through sooner rather than later.

"Doing this before the job is totally finished might upset the client," says Jonathan Cleveland of Boston-based Cleveland Design. "So I say to a client,

> 'Of course you may need some final tweaks, which we will bill separately at a later date. And if they come up, I will be sure to give you an estimate for additional work.'

"This is especially necessary when doing websites. There are always follow-up issues, and I don't want the client to think that those issues were included in the final invoice we sent them a month before."

## WHEN PAYMENT IS LATE

Many creative professionals again prefer to wait rather than "confront" the client about an unpaid invoice. But it's not a confrontation, especially if you refrain from making any assumptions about what happened. Instead, approach it with curiosity. Don't you want to know what happened to your invoice? Begin by asking what they know.

Maybe your invoice was lost, which can happen easily when you submit them via e-mail rather than the old-fashioned, paper-based way. It's not a bad idea to do both. Or, if that's confusing to your client, ask them to confirm receipt of your invoice when you send it.

The first time a client's payment is late, call or write to find out what's going on. Don't jump to any conclusions and don't imply they've done something to avoid paying. Always make it sound like something is beyond their control, almost sympathetically.

> "Probably someone over in accounting mislaid the invoice or maybe it slipped behind the file cabinet."

Or,

> "Can you ask whoever's in charge of those things to have a look at it?"

Or you can be more direct. When a client is late with payment, Cleveland sends a PDF of the invoice with a quick note that says,

> "Hi there, can you check on the status of this invoice for me? It's a few days late and I just wanted to make sure it is on the way to us."

If you sense it's due to a cash-flow problem, handle it in a straightforward manner. If your client is being vague and systematically avoiding your queries about money, don't give them an opportunity to ignore you. Ask explicitly about it:

> "We're moving ahead but we really need to get our act together on the money side."

Emphasize "us," since you're in it together.

If this doesn't work in writing, use the phone. Your approach should not be antagonistic. Don't add to their pressure with anything that smacks of, "I need my money. I don't care what's happening on your end," even if that's how you feel. Instead, position yourself as a sympathetic ally. Find a way to empathize with the situation you imagine they are in, which is harder to do when you barely know them. Try to pick up on something you guess might be the source of their unease. Try phrases like:

> "I can see that money might not be on your hot list of topics on this project and I'm sensing that maybe you're in a bit of a squeeze."
>
> "Maybe it's a tougher sell to the VPs than we thought?"
>
> "I can imagine things are really tough around there …"

If you don't have enough information, you can simply empathize about being overwhelmed, since that's a problem for almost everyone.

> "You're probably totally swamped with that other project you've been talking about, but on the mundane admin side of our project, we still haven't gotten this figured out."
>
> "I know you're still catching up on two thousand e-mails from that trip out west, but one of those messages was about our invoice."

Be careful not to sound insincere. Try to let them see that you are sympathetic. You help them through the awkwardness of having been asked more than once and not responding. You provide their excuse but you don't let them off the hook. They save face and you've accomplished your objective.

## HOW LONG TO WAIT BEFORE YOU TAKE ACTION

Most important in these situations is to keep the lines of communication open and to stay levelheaded. Which actions you take depend on many factors, including why nonpayment is happening, where you are in the process of the project and how much you value the relationship.

Assuming the terms in your contract—approved or signed by your client— are 30–45 days, after that, they are officially late. However, in a slow economy, 60–90 days can be "normal." Here are some guidelines to follow with large companies or organizations:

**At 45–60 days:** Be patient but not passive, especially if you're dealing with a solid corporation and you know they are good for it, or if there was a screw up and the invoice got into the system weeks late. Know who the point person is for payment and give them a nudge. Keep working on their project.

**At 60–90 days:** Be persistent but don't nag. Big corporations definitely warrant a nudge past 60 days, as the invoice may still be sitting unapproved on someone's desk. Start calling the accounts payable department to find out what else you may need to do. Stay in touch and be careful about deliverables.

**Past 90 days:** This is actually pretty common. Don't be strident and risk losing a good account because you can't tolerate their bureaucratic lapses. Enlist the help of your client's project manager to find out what's going on with their accounting department and state clearly that you won't be able to deliver the work if you aren't paid. The pressure they can apply might do the trick.

A slightly different approach is warranted when your client is a small company and your contact wears all the hats, including accounting. Don't make it the most important aspect of the project but don't ignore it either. Find out what's going on and get a commitment about when you can expect payment. If you aren't confident you'll be paid, withhold deliverables until you are paid. Stay professional at all times and don't take it personally.

If their solvency is questionable, your attitude shifts from, "I'm sympathetic" to, "This is a problem." Be persistent and firm but not aggressive. Avoid declarations, such as "This is outrageous." No matter what, don't go postal.

## WHEN THE CLIENT REFUSES TO PAY

This is not the norm. Most people are honest and most companies are working in good faith. It's just that things happen; people and companies fall on hard times. That's what contracts are for, to protect you in case you don't see it coming. Here's what you can do:

1. **Remain professional and don't stress.** Most important is to deal with these situations rationally. If you feel angry or emotional, wait until your head is clear

before you have any contact with the client. Don't put anything in writing that could damage your reputation.

2. **Stop work.** If you are still working on any projects, stop immediately and let the client know you'll be happy to resume when payment is resolved. This is not a punishment; your paying clients come first.

3. **Be squeaky.** Call and e-mail every week, even every day. They are likely to pay you just to stop the harassment.

4. **Offer other payment options.** If you haven't already, suggest other payment options, such as a credit card (let the bank await payment), PayPal or a bank transfer.

5. **Offer a payment plan.** Try to get them to agree to pay you by a certain time. A deadline gives you a boundary to work within.

6. **Charge late fees.** If you haven't mentioned this up front, you can't just slap them on as a punishment and expect them to be paid (although sometimes they are). If you really want to charge late fees, it needs to be discussed during negotiations, included in your payment terms and repeated on your invoice.

7. **Send a personal letter.** Use certified mail to indicate you are serious and state that using your work without payment means they are in violation of copyright, with or without a contract. This hints at the legal ramifications without being threatening and can be just enough to convince them you would be more trouble than you're worth.

**8. Get a letter from your lawyer.** If a personal appeal isn't feasible, have your lawyer write a letter. But keep in mind that a corporate lawyer may be expensive, and you risk eating through whatever's owed to you quickly.

**9. Show up in person.** If they are dodging your calls and e-mail messages, you may have no choice but to show up in the office. The best approach here is to appeal to their humanity, almost forcing them into your shoes. Describe your situation so they can't help but agree. Say,

> "I think you can appreciate the situation I'm in. I understand your predicament but what would you do in my shoes?"

Who's going to say no to that? That changes the conversation and can be effective with reasonable people.

**10. Advise next steps but don't make empty threats.** Let them know you'll be calling a collections agency (some charge only a minimal fee to recover the funds) and reporting them to the Better Business Bureau. A collections agency will affect their credit, and BBB will affect their community status. You might also be able to file a complaint with your local chamber of commerce.

**11. Take them to small-claims court.** Almost everyone has an opinion (and a story) about whether taking a client to small-claims court is worth the time and money. Some say it will cost more than the project is worth and you'll never win; others say it doesn't cost much (it varies from state to state in the United States) and is worth it, if only on principle. This is a personal decision and should be decided case by case.

Jonathan Cleveland tells of taking a client to small-claims court once: "I had a contract, they had a printed brochure. I won very easily."

## WRITE IT OFF?

It's important to distinguish between the situations that are most valuable as "lessons learned" and those that are worth fighting for. They can be very valuable lessons, teaching everything from the unpredictability of business to the importance of adhering to your professional policies. Take your lumps and move on.

In most cases, you'll do better to write off bad accounts, especially the small ones. Unless the sums involved are significant, you may waste more time trying to collect than the invoice is worth. It's a more positive use of time and energy to focus on new business development than chasing down bad debt. In some cases, you may receive payment months or years later.

Much of this can be avoided by not ignoring red flags early on and making sure you establish—and adhere to—standard business policies regarding advance payments and contracts. You can usually weed out the bad seeds through that process and avoid the headaches later on.

Ideally, the longer you are in business, the better you get (and the more confident you are) about handling these situations.

Maybe next time it will be easier to ask for that deposit.

# PART THREE

---

# HOW TO MANAGE IT

---

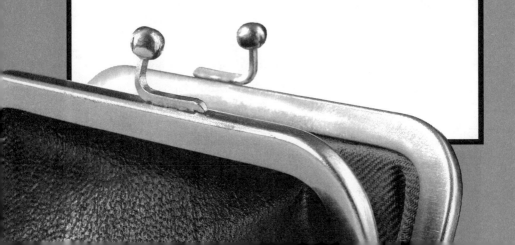

## SELF ASSESSMENT: WHAT ARE YOUR THOUGHTS ON MANAGING MONEY?

- I don't know how much I need to live on.
- I can't save money because I never know how much is coming in.
- I put off my taxes until the last minute.
- I don't know how much I earned until I do my taxes.
- I put someone else in charge of my financial situation.
- I have never reconciled a bank account.
- When people start talking about numbers, my mind glazes over.
- I think it's time to get serious about how I manage my financial situation.

If you checked off several of the boxes above, you may be tempted to skip this section of the book. Don't.

This is where we get to the nitty-gritty. In this final section, the goal is to focus on the areas creative professionals struggle with the most, clear up any common misconceptions and point you to more detailed information and resources so you can get a handle on your finances.

# CHAPTER 11
# MONEY BASICS

"I'm surprised how many creative professionals don't know how much they make."

—GALIA GICHON, AUTHOR OF
THE "MY MONEY MATTERS" KIT

Do you know what you owe, what you own, what you spend and what you earn? According to Galia Gichon, owner of New York-based consulting practice Down-to-Earth Finance and author of the *My Money Matters Kit*, you should know these numbers off the top of your head. If you don't, you may be walking around in a numbers fog.

How easy it is to look the other way... yet how important to look at where you are. You may think you know how your business is doing but unless you have the numbers in front of you, you can't be sure. What you're actually earning and what "it feels like you're earning" are two very different things. The facts may surprise you. Even if it's bad news, it's better to know the facts than to stay in the fog. Otherwise, you can't do anything to remedy the situation.

Says Gichon, "Aren't you working really hard? And for what? Don't you want to own your home or go on a vacation you've paid cash for or simply stop worrying about money? You have to want it bad enough."

Planning is the key, and you must know what you'll do when things change—as they always do. "When the money slows to a trickle, as it is bound to do from time to time, you don't need to panic. Instead you'll have a plan," says Gichon. "You'll have already thought through how to handle it." That's the place to start: where you are right now.

To hear an interview with Galia Gichon, go to www.creative freelancerblog.com /money-guide.

---

# DO YOU KNOW YOUR NUMBERS?

One of the challenges for creative professionals is the commingling of business and personal. If your personal finances are not in order, it's a pretty sure bet your business finances aren't either.

You should know where you stand financially—off the top of your head. If you don't right now, fill out this simple form. Do it every month until you don't have to anymore. Do it for both personal and business. You'll be surprised how much more calm you'll feel when armed with this basic information about your current situation, even if the news isn't great.

## PERSONAL FINANCES

How much do you owe (all debts, including your mortgage)?

How much do you own (all savings, investments, home equity, etc.)?

---

How much do you spend (what is your total monthly spending)?

How much do you earn (what is your average monthly income)?

## BUSINESS FINANCES

Some of these numbers may be elusive because they vary from month to month. But take an average so you have something to work with.

How much do you owe (your liabilities, including outstanding bills to vendors and credit card bills)?

How much do you own (your assets, cash on hand, all equipment, etc.)?

How much do you spend (what is your average monthly overhead)?

How much do you earn (what is your average monthly revenue)?

## WHAT YOU CAN CONTROL

The point of being self-employed is to be in control of more of your life, and yet so many people don't take control of their finances, one of the few things you actually *can* control.

Galia Gichon agrees. "You can't control the economy or the stock market, but you can control your money," says Gichon. "The secret is working as hard to manage it as you do to earn it—and not getting overwhelmed by important things like budgets, cash flow and saving for retirement."

So realistically, what can you control?

1. **Your fixed expenses.** You roll out of bed, as they say, and you still have to pay the fixed expenses. On the personal side, that's rent or mortgage, utilities and day care. On the business side, it's phone and Internet, rent, maybe transportation. These don't change from one month to the next, although there is a lot you can do to reduce them.

2. **Your variable expenses.** For personal, it's usually groceries, entertainment and travel. For business, it's everything it takes to keep your computer humming (software and hardware) and the projects rolling in and out (marketing and networking, professional development, travel and entertainment). These expenses are entirely within your control.

3. **Your debt.** When used strategically, debt can help you grow. It can also get easily out of hand. When you control your debt, you know how much you can afford to charge to a credit card and you don't charge impulsively. If you've used credit cards to finance your business, you should have a plan to pay them off. With large purchases—for equipment or conferences—take time to think first about the expected return on your investment and how you will generate the work to pay it off.

**4. Your cash flow.** Maintaining a healthy cash flow is within your control but it does take some controlling. Cash flow tends to be a problem for creative professionals who don't bill in a timely manner and/or who advance money for client expenses without being reimbursed in a timely manner. Even if you do all the right things, you can expect a cash crunch from time to time, but as long as you have some money in reserve, you'll barely feel the crunch.

**5. Your reserves.** Aim to put away three months of fixed business expenses for the next cash-flow crunch. And create two spending plans: one with a monthly spending amount that allows you to build your business when cash is flowing abundantly, and one for difficult times, which addresses the bare bones of what you must bring in to the keep the doors open.

## What Kind of Financial Help Do You Need?

Do you need a bookkeeper, financial advisor, accountant or all three? Do some professionals fill more than one of those roles?

### You Definitely Need an Accountant

If you have nothing else, you should have an accountant. According to Cameron Foote, author of *The Creative Business Guide to Running a Graphic Design Business*, "Every business needs an outside, objective analyst to help it follow standard financial operating procedures and make important financial decisions. In addition, tax obligations of the simplest enterprise today are much too complex for even interested and knowledgeable principals to handle themselves. Rules change quickly, often without public notice, and the price for not following them to the letter can be steep."

When choosing an accountant, look for a small firm or solo practitioner who specializes in small businesses and, if possible, in creative businesses like yours. Don't be impressed by prestigious firms; they won't have the specialized knowledge you need. "You are looking for someone who is fundamentally different than you," writes Foote. "Someone who is much more detail- and process-oriented. Choose someone with whom you feel comfortable talking and to whom you can disclose confidential information. You must be comfortable enough to freely question your accountant so that you understand the reasoning behind their advice because, ultimately, it is you who is held responsible for any tax or accounting mistakes, not your accountant."

"The more knowledgeable your accountant is about your day-to-day operations, the more specific and helpful his or her advice will be. Meet at least twice a year with your accountant, once to do tax preparation and again in the middle of the year for a business review or update to go over any changes that might affect your taxes or financial planning."

### It Helps to Have a Banker on Your Side

No matter the size of your business, in order to keep the boundaries clear for yourself, you should have a separate business account into which you deposit all business payments and from which you pay all business-related expenses. This is not required for tax purposes but it will keep your process simpler, especially if you are doing business under a company name.

Even if you prefer to do your day-to-day banking online, take the time to develop a relationship with the banker where your business account is held. Introduce yourself to the bank manager, instead of a teller or other staff member. The manager will see that you are taken seriously and your concerns are addressed. Make a point to physically go into the same branch so the staff knows who you are and you know who's in charge, in case you ever need help.

The branch manager can pave the way if you need a credit line or loan to grow your business. As your business grows, so do your financial needs, such as merchant (credit card payment) and payroll services, 401K plans, linked accounts and more. Since most banks offer similar services, make your choice based on convenience, friendliness, customer service and responsiveness.

### A Bookkeeper Can Provide an Extra Set of Eyes

The essentials of bookkeeping are neither difficult nor inherently confusing. It's just a matter of training your mind to focus on the details. The task is essentially to put all your financial data (bills paid and money received) in order so that you can see your entire financial picture at the push of a button.

You can hire a professional bookkeeper who understands creative businesses to set you up to do it yourself or to come in regularly to take care of basic tasks for you. Either way, it's a good idea to have an independent set of eyes on your finances.

Technology has made almost everything related to bookkeeping a cinch. Between online banking; bookkeeping software such as Quicken or QuickBooks; and online budgeting tools, such as what you'll find at Mint.com, there's no longer any excuse.

All you have to do is input the information into any one of these automated programs so an accountant can prepare your taxes. (Ask your accountant which accounting program to use, as you will need to export the files in a compatible format.) You don't even have to do most of the number-crunching. The computer does it for you!

Here is what a live person needs to do:

For more accounting and bookkeeping resources, go to www.creativefreelancerblog.com/money-guide.

1. **Keep everything in one place, literally.** Most of the confusion surrounding business bookkeeping is a result of fragmentation—all the bits of paper and electronically stored information scattered everywhere. To avoid that, keep everything related to your finances in a money drawer or box or file folder: an electronic one on your computer and a physical one near your desk. Put all receipts, invoices, check stubs, bank statements and anything related to money in one place so you can attend to it when it's time. Keep all receipts and make the extra effort to notate what you are doing and with whom, especially if it's business related. That way, you won't have to use your imperfect memory (or your imagination) later.

2. **Input the data.** You shouldn't need more than a few hours per month to import or input any data from online and/or offline checking, invoices and receipts. Be sure to have a block of undisturbed time when you can spread out and get organized, one morning when your mind is clear or one evening when the house is quiet.

**3. Reconcile monthly.** You will sleep much easier if you don't ignore your bank statements, whether you get them on paper or electronically. Take the time to do the reconciliation to make sure you have what they have. Question any unknown or miscellaneous charges. Banks aren't infallible and they are known to pile on the charges when you're not watching.

**4. Budget.** Bookkeeping software should assist you in creating a budget of what you plan to earn and spend in your business. With numbers on paper, you can anticipate how much money you will have available if things continue as they are or if they change, up or down, and you can adjust your spending and marketing accordingly. That way, you are free to attend to your creative work.

**5. Watch the trends.** Is your income rising year after year? Is there a seasonal aspect to your business that is obvious from a year-to-year comparison? Is there a pattern to your spending or to your income that you can use to project for the future? The trends are more important than the details of any particularly good or bad month. (Much more about this in Chapter 12: Profitability and Metrics.) You can see what is owed on an average monthly basis and you'll know what you must earn to cover this amount. Watching the trends in your business will allow you to predict and prepare for slow periods, whether you use that time to take a vacation, for professional development or for a major marketing campaign.

Whether you crunch the numbers yourself or someone else does it for you, as a business owner you must keep your own eyes on your finances, learning enough about basic accounting so you know what to look for.

## Which Business Expenses Can You Deduct?

One of the well-known tax benefits of being self-employed in the United States is the ability to deduct business expenses, which lowers the income on which you pay taxes and thereby lowers your taxes.

But which business expenses count? Here is the definition of a business expense according to the U.S. Internal Revenue Service: Business expenses are the cost of carrying on a trade or business. These expenses are usually deductible if the business is operated to make a profit.

In other words, if you intend to make a profit—investing money in a business is evidence of that intention—the money you spend toward that end can be considered a business expense, even if you don't actually make a profit.

As for which business expenses are deductible, the IRS says, "To be deductible, a business expense must be both ordinary and necessary. An ordinary expense is one that is common and accepted in your field of business. A necessary expense is one that is appropriate and helpful for your business. An expense does not have to be indispensable to be considered necessary."

These are very broad definitions that leave a lot of room for interpretation. That's a good thing. In her book, *Self-Employed Tax Solutions*, June Walker writes, "Anything you do that relates to your work, that stimulates or enhances your business, nurtures your professional creativity, improves your skills, wins you recognition, or increases your chances of making a sale is a business expense and therefore deductible."

So as long as you can make a strong case for how each expense is ordinary and necessary for your business, you can quite legitimately deduct it. For the best tax advantage, Walker recommends defining your business as broadly and as honestly as possible. So a generalist writer who writes on a variety of topics can deduct more than a medical writer who only writes about the medical field.

Also, a creative professional who specializes in the entertainment industry can legitimately spend and deduct all entertainment-related expenses, such as tickets to movies and theatre productions, purchases of DVDs, even the purchase of the latest console or home entertainment unit. Likewise, a designer looking to break into the computer game market can deduct as "research" any games he or she buys (and plays).

Walker also writes in her book about adopting an "indie mind-set," which allows you to see your relationships differently and consider the possible business connections that may exist between you and anyone you encounter in both your professional and personal life. So if you chat with another parent on the playground and he or she refers you to someone who becomes a client, any expenses you incur related to that parent—such as coffee and donuts while the children play—could be deductible as a business expense. Likewise, a videographer targeting the high-tech market can deduct the cost of a dinner spent picking the brain of a friend in that industry, even if they don't do business together.

Where it can get a little tricky is when it comes to expenses that have both a business and personal use. Here's what the IRS says about that: Generally, you cannot deduct personal, living, or family expenses. However, if you have an expense for something that is used partly for business and partly for personal purposes, divide the total cost between the business and personal parts. You can deduct the business part. If you use part of your home for business, you may be able to deduct expenses for the business use of your home. These expenses may include mortgage interest, insurance, utilities, repairs, and depreciation.

There is a wealth of easy-to-understand information on this at www.irs.gov. For more on business expenses, go to www.creative freelancerblog.com /money-guide.

For creative professionals, the other tricky issue can be dealing with reimbursed expenses—that is, an expense you pay for on behalf of your client and are later reimbursed for. There is no right way to handle this but Walker prefers the simple way. When you bill a client for a $3,500 creative fee plus $10,000 in printing expenses, simply claim the entire $13,500 as income and $10,000 is a business expense (which is, of course, deductible). Simply note the difference on the deposit slip for your own reference. This way, at the end of the year, your deposits match up.

The only potential problem is if you live in a state that taxes gross income. The reimbursed expenses are not part of your gross income so you'll need to have a separate tally to differentiate the income for state tax purposes so your tax professional can address that at the end of the year.

## How Long to Keep Tax Records

Do you ever wonder how long you have to keep all that paper around in case of an audit? June Walker says, "Contrary to popular opinion, people don't usually get into trouble by not saving records. They do run into problems by saving the wrong ones, outdated ones or too many different records—or by not knowing where the right ones are. The huge stack of papers in the attic is often there due to inertia caused by not knowing which records need to be kept and which can be tossed."

Walker suggests that you:

- Keep forever: tax returns—not all the backup, but the actual returns you send to the IRS and every year-end summary of your pension.

- Keep for seven years from the last time it had any impact on your financial life: everything else.

According to Walker, most audits take place within two years of the time you file your return. "However, if you unknowingly (that is, not intentionally) neglect to include at least 25 percent of your income on your return then the statute of limitations is extended from three years after filing to six years after filing. (That's seven years from the time of the transaction.)"

## Are You "Saving Up"?

Most of us grew up with a piggy bank, and some of us experienced the thrill of saving up for that really cool new toy or game or even a car. But somewhere along the line, our culture seems to have lost its taste for saving money. Now saving requires a tremendous amount of structure and discipline in order to accomplish, especially for creative professionals. It wasn't always like this.

Your great-grandmother probably had a few envelopes in a drawer in the dining room. Maybe you came across them one day while snooping around. Each had a word or phrase on it, "groceries" or "rent," and inside was cash. This was how people saved money back in the day. And it worked quite well.

Experts today recommend the electronic equivalent: instead of envelopes in a drawer, you use a few different bank accounts. That way, when a check comes in, you immediately divide it into the various buckets. Here are some buckets to consider:

- **Taxes:** Whatever your tax bracket, deduct that percentage and transfer it right away. If you don't know, you'll be safe with something between 20–30%

- **Fixed expenses:** Based on what you know you must spend each month, put a percentage of each check toward that number so you have it when you need it.

- **Short-term savings:** Put a little money away for a rainy day. You never know when you'll need it. Even if it's a small amount, whether $25 or $100, developing the habit is what's important.

- **Discretionary spending:** Give yourself an amount to spend and decide what's important: whether it's $50, $250 or $1,000, don't spend more than you allocate. What counts is adhering to a limit and practicing discipline.

In *The Money Book for Freelancers, Part-Timers and the Self-Employed,* Joseph D'Agnese and Denise Kiernan, both veteran freelancers and journalists, write, "Most Americans—freelancers or not—do a terrible job of saving for the future. Scratch that. Most people do a lousy job of saving, period. They assume that the future will simply be a continuation of the present. But that just isn't true. Despite the multivitamins you swallow, the carbs you shun, or the reps you crank out at the gym, someday you will probably get too old to work. And you won't see any more checks except the canceled ones you wrote yourself lying at the bottom of your desk drawer.

"Why don't many people achieve this goal? They make lots of mistakes. They wait too long to start saving. They save inconsistently: a lot this year, too little the next. Or they are stuck in a pattern of denial: Why do I need to save for retirement? I'm only [insert age here]. I have time to save."

Their book recommends a strategy similar to your great-grandmother's. They call it the Freelance Finance system. With lots of charts and graphs for the visually oriented, they outline a system with separate accounts keyed to your major financial goals and show how to determine the percentages associated with each.

Find Hugh Chou's program here: www .creativefreelancerblog .com/money-guide.

After reading *The Money Book*, computer programmer Hugh Chou created a simple program to calculate how much you should be saving for emergency, taxes and retirement.

### Saving for Retirement

You will most probably need a bucket for retirement too. There are many factors involved in determining what percentages you should be saving, but if you've never done it before, start small. Setting aside 3, 4 or 5 percent is fine. Or start with $100 a month. It's never too soon to start saving. And don't wait until all your debt is paid off. Galia Gichon emphasizes the importance of saving for retirement and believes it can and should be done while paying off debt. It will just take longer. Start with whatever you can and build from there. You can always increase once you get the hang of it.

As for retirement plans, Gichon suggests looking first at self-employed retirement plans like a SEP IRA, which can be opened at any mutual fund company. The SEP IRA is the most popular plan for self-employed individuals and small business owners thanks to its high annual contribution limits, discretionary and flexible annual contributions and minimal administration. SEP IRA plans can be established by any one-person business or by a business owner with employees. Sole proprietorships, S and C corporations, partnerships and LLCs all qualify.

If you don't have enough to fund the complete IRA, consider setting up an automatic transfer to your Roth or Traditional IRA. Writes Gichon, "The Roth IRA is an individual retirement account with special tax benefits. Your contributions are made with after-tax dollars and it grows tax-deferred. When you start withdrawing the money at age 59½, it is tax-free. A great benefit of the Roth IRA is that if the principal has been in the account for at least five years, there is no penalty to take the money out. There is also no penalty if it is used for a first-time home purchase, qualified education expense or certain medical hardships."

## How's Your Credit Rating?

Did you know that your personal credit rating affects your business? If you apply for a loan or even rent office space, they will check your credit or "FICO" score, so make sure it's clean. Here's how:

- **Find out your credit score.** This is what banks and creditors are looking at to evaluate how much money you can borrow and at what interest rate. The higher your score, the lower your interest on all loans, including credit cards and mortgages. The highest and best rating is 850.

- **Get your score from each of the three credit bureaus.** Experian, Equifax and TransUnion are the big three. Check all three because they have been known to make mistakes. Verify that your personal information is correct and that the debts noted are indeed yours. Also, look for any duplicate information or resolved debts that may still be listed.

Find all these resources at www.creative freelancerblog.com /money-guide.

- **Keep your credit report clean.** Every time you apply for a new credit card, a business loan or buy or refinance a home, an inquiry is made to your credit report. Multiple inquiries to your credit report will lower your FICO score.

## CONTROL YOUR HABITS

Even if you've gotten this far without learning basic financial skills, it's not too late. Now is a great time to learn and to set better habits.

1. **Create a money day.** Galia Gichon suggests designating one day of the week to take care of and organize your financial commitments. You don't have to use the whole day for this, but be sure to use this day to pay

bills, update your personal finance software, make any necessary transfers, get cash, check your balances and, when it's time, reconcile your bank accounts. It's best to do all of this at the same time in a focused frame of mind.

2. **Open all financial mail the day it arrives.** Set it aside so it doesn't get lost in a pile of junk mail. Don't put off opening and reading any relevant statements.

3. **Pay your bills right away.** Don't wait until the due date or you may forget, which is the beginning of the end when it comes to ruining your credit.

4. **Pay as many bills as possible online.** This saves time, money and stress. Set up automatic payments for recurring charges so you don't forget to pay. This will help keep your credit intact.

Taking responsibility for—and taking care of—your finances is one important way to take care of yourself. Don't let it wait for a crisis point. Make it a priority now. Here's how:

1. **Get organized.** See where you are today and where you want to be. Separate personal from business. Find one place for all those pieces of paper. And don't keep them longer than you have to.

2. **Get realistic.** Think small. Divide the tasks into bite-sized pieces and schedule them into your day/week/month. That way, it's not a big mountain to climb, but rather a few slopes, one after another.

**3. Get serious.** It's easy to say, "It's too hard. I can't do it." But what do you know? Have you tried?

**4. Get the tools you need.** Get the software and use it. Find a bookkeeper to do it for you or hire one to tutor you.

**5. Get help.** Don't do it alone. Take a class. Find a friend. Read a book with a friend. We're not meant to do all these things alone. Having others involved gives you some perspective, not to mention accountability.

# CHAPTER 12
# PROFITABILITY AND METRICS

"I've known friends who get so engrossed in the work for clients that they have a hot mess of financial records. I have found that I have to actually schedule in time on my calendar as if it were a project for a client to devote to my accounting/finances so that I always know how much I'm bringing in, spending, and what I need to do to get more projects coming in to keep the bills paid."

**—JOSHUA MILLER, COMMENTING
ON THE MARKETING MIX BLOG**

Here's where things become challenging for creative professionals who profess not to be "business people." This chapter begins with simple definitions, then proceeds with increasingly more technical detail and business jargon. Read as far as you like, according to how much you want to know.

## PROFITABILITY AND METRICS: WHAT DO THOSE WORDS MEAN?

Let's start with some basic definitions.

**Profitability:** If your profit is your total income for the year, less the expenses you paid out, then your profitability is determined not by how much money flowed into your bank account but by what was left over at the end of the day.

In other words, you may have been frightfully busy this year and deposited the biggest checks of your career, but not have much to show for it—very little or no profit. This is often a result of not charging enough or over-delivering on projects with low fees. So achieving profitability lies in finding the clients who can pay you enough to make a healthy profit, whether you choose to sock that money away, reinvest it in the business or spend it lavishly.

**Metrics:** A profitable business is a healthy business, and metrics are the measurements that you use to take the temperature of your business to determine its health. Successful businesses use metrics or "industry benchmarks" to compare their performance year over year and to that of others in the industry. Tracking these metrics and analyzing the trends over time—not just annually at tax time—is essential if your goal is long-term success rather than riding a precarious wave of luck.

But if your aim is simply to make a living and live a stress-free life doing something you love, you don't need to know everything about profitability and you may not even need metrics. It's up to you.

## TRACK YOUR INCOME; BALLPARK YOUR EXPENSES (OR, THE MINIMUM YOU NEED TO KNOW AND DO)

What do you really need to track the money in your business? What systems do you need to have in place? What software, if any, should you be using? What reports should you be running?

June Walker says it depends on what you're comfortable with, and she's surprisingly lenient when it comes to what a creative professional should be doing. In reality, most people wearing all the hats in their own business are not doing monthly record keeping and don't want to. "That's usually fine," says Walker, "unless your state requires you to."

Good point: Record keeping is done for two reasons. You keep records for taxes and also for your own psychological well-being. What you do for yourself may not be comprehensive or detailed enough for your taxes. For example, if your state requires that you collect and pay sales tax, you must have a handle on your gross income on a monthly or quarterly basis. Therefore, you must keep your records up to date monthly so you can determine how much money is owed to the state monthly or quarterly. If your state doesn't require it, you can do as much as will keep you stress free on a day-to-day basis.

No matter what your state requires, for your own sanity, you at least need to know your income—gross (before expenses) and net (after expenses but before taxes)—especially if you want to anticipate and avoid a cash crunch.

Simply keep a record of your total income by listing each payment as you receive it, whether by check, credit card or cash. You can do this on a spreadsheet, using bookkeeping software or on a piece of paper tacked on the refrigerator. The trick is to make it easy and to develop the discipline to do it every single time.

You also need to know a ballpark estimate of your monthly expenses. This does not have to be exact, but rather an average of what you spend over a six- to twelve-month period. With those two pieces of information, you can determine your net income, otherwise known as your profit. But that's not what you take home. You still have to subtract up to 40 percent for taxes.

Here's the simple math: Gross income minus expenses equals net income, of which 40 percent goes to taxes.

So, if you made $20,000 total (gross) and have an average of $5,000 in deductible expenses, then $15,000 is your net income and 40 percent of that—$6,000—belongs to the government. "You can't spend the net income. It's not all yours," Walker emphasizes. "That's the most important thing. Take that 40 percent and put it aside for your estimated taxes, under the mattress, in another checking or savings account. You can even send it off to the government early if that will prevent you from spending it."

## Figuring Your Estimated Taxes

One reason to track your current income is to anticipate how much you'll owe at the end of the year, rather than be surprised when your tax professional presents your finished tax returns. For your own well-being, it may be a good idea to track that, especially if the mention of taxes makes you nervous.

However, this year's income is not what you use to figure how much you owe for this year's estimated taxes. This year's estimated taxes are based on last year's income, while this year's income will be used to determine next year's estimated taxes. So if you earned $100,000 last year, you'd be paying up to $40,000 (or $10,000 per quarter) this year, even if this year you are on track to double your income and earn $200,000. That won't affect your estimated taxes until next year, when your taxes will at least double.

## Track Who Owes You Money

Your life will be calmer—and your cash flow smoother—if you also track who owes you money. As with income received, every time you send an invoice, jot it down on an ongoing list with the date you expect to be paid, based on what you agreed to with your client. (And be sure to follow up if you don't receive it by that time. It's easy to get behind in your collections process, and it is detrimental to your cash flow to have money outstanding.)

### Basic Record Keeping: Manual or Electronic?

Whether you're keeping simple records for yourself or more detailed records for the government, how you do it is up to you. You can do it on paper or on the computer. There is no right way. If you prefer the simple way, create simple worksheets for yourself like the ones below:

June Walker explains a simple manual system for record-keeping in her book, *Self-Employed Tax Solutions*, with more detail and worksheets in "The Confident Indie" and "5 Easy Steps," which are available on her website, www .junewalkeronline.com.

### INCOME FOR _____ (YEAR)

| DATE | CLIENT | AMOUNT | NOTES |
|------|--------|--------|-------|
| 5/25/11 | ABC company/ brochure | $2,000.00 | Deposit |

| DATE | CLIENT | AMOUNT | NOTES |
|------|--------|--------|-------|
| 5/30/11 | XYZ website | $5,000.00 | Phase 2 |
| 5/30/11 | Trade show booth for Acme | $431.00 | Final expenses |
| | | | |
| | | | |
| | | | |
| | | | |
| | | | |
| | | | |
| | | | |
| | | | |
| | TOTAL | | |

## EXPENSES FOR _____ (MONTH)

| DATE | CLIENT | AMOUNT | CATEGORY | NOTES |
|------|--------|--------|----------|-------|
| 5/22/11 | XYX Corp. | $357.41 | Travel | Airline ticket for kickoff meeting |
| 5/31/11 | Labworks | $123.89 | Phone | Monthly, check #333 |
| | | | | |
| | | | | |
| | | | | |
| | | | | |
| | | | | |
| | | | | |
| | | | | |
| TOTAL | | | | |

## Do You Need Bookkeeping Software?

The simple answer is no, you don't need fancy software to do any of this. But if you are going to use software (and it does make your life easier), Walker recommends Quicken because it is just like your checking account and is designed for "the layman."

Many self-employed people use QuickBooks because of its invoicing capabilities (which Quicken doesn't have), but it is a double entry system that is designed for accountants. You only need that if you have a bookkeeper or accountant on staff to do your bookkeeping and/or your tax professional recommends it. For invoicing, there are much better systems and resources available, such as FreshBooks, a favorite among freelancers. (See the Resources section for more recommendations.)

Quicken can also help you track your expenses by project or by client to see how much you spent on each project. If your business finances are mingled with your personal ones, Walker recommends inputting everything, personal and business accounts, savings accounts—even your spouse's checking account—to get a realistic sense of how much you're spending. Analysis is only useful if the information is accurate and complete.

Those are the basics. If you want to know more, learn a bit of the jargon and stretch your business mind, read on. If not, skip to the next chapter.

## ACCOUNTING REPORTS (OR, MORE DETAILS ON WHAT YOU NEED TO KNOW AND DO)

The most important and fundamental reports, which you can generate using all basic bookkeeping software (including Quicken and QuickBooks) are:

- Income statements, also called P/L or Profit and Loss statements
- Accounts payable, which includes all bills you have outstanding
- Accounts receivable, which includes all invoices you have outstanding

### Your Income Statement (a.k.a. Profit and Loss)

The name "Profit and Loss" is actually one point of confusion with this report, which is essentially a listing of your income and expenses. It will show a profit if you took in more than you spent during the allotted time period, and it will show a loss if you spent more than you took in. So it's actually a report of *either* profit or loss. And it's a fancy (i.e. electronic) way of tracking what was tracked manually on the previous pages.

This is the report to review monthly. It tells you where your money is coming from and where it's going, so you can stay on track and, ideally, generate a profit every month.

The income statement represents a period of time of your choosing. You can look at year-to-date or month-to-date or you can compare this month last year to this month this year. For the specified time frame, it collects your revenues and details your expenses (not including taxes, unless they were paid during the time period), leaving you with your net income (a.k.a. profit).

Review your income statement (P/L) monthly to see:

- All revenue (or gross income) = all your sales, minus what you paid contractors for jobs you marked up

- All operating expenses (or costs) = bills you pay, including rent, utilities, travel and entertainment, payroll, payroll taxes, etc.

- Profits (or net income) = what's left over after you subtract expenses from income

If you track this report regularly, you can see mid-month, for example, just how slow a slow month is, and decide to forego an unnecessary purchase or cut back a freelancer's hours. You can't accurately make these quick decisions without the data provided by the income statement.

## TYPICAL BUSINESS EXPENSE CATEGORIES

| | |
|---|---|
| Advertising/promotion | Equipment |
| Auto expenses | Internet/phone |
| Bank charges | Legal and professional services |
| Business gifts | Licenses and permit fees |
| Business insurance | Meals/entertainment |
| Commissions and fees | Office supplies |
| Dues and subscriptions | Other supplies |

| Rent | Transportation (commuting) |
| Repairs/maintenance | Travel (trips) |
| Research | Utilities |
| Sub-contractor fees | Wages paid |
| Taxes (business) | |

## Your Accounts Payable and Receivable

What you owe (accounts payable) and what you are owed (accounts receivable) are the heart of your cash flow, and you should have a handle on this at all times. If you have input all the data for the income statement (outstanding invoices and checks to pay), you can easily generate the basic accounts payable and accounts receivable reports at the click of a button using any software.

More helpful is a report called Accounts Receivable Aging Summary, which tracks how quickly your customers pay your company and shows both small and large receivables at a glance so you can determine which to follow up on first. (See Chapter 10: Getting Paid for details on how to follow up). There is no right or wrong amount of time to get paid, and this amount is also affected by the economy. Thirty to sixty days is typical for most companies to pay a bill, though some stretch it longer if they can.

You should know (or will quickly learn) what's normal for your business and for each client—and you can have a hand in determining that, if you are clear and firm about your payment policies. Beware, however, if you always have a high balance in your accounts receivable (i.e. lots of bills outstanding for more than an accepted amount of time), it may mean your customers are essentially using you as a bank. Instead of formally borrowing money, they simply pay you late. That's not right.

To track the bills you have to pay and how long you've been holding them, generate a report called Accounts Payable Aging Summary. Note that it lists whom you must pay, not which expense was incurred. For example, a bill from Verizon is obviously for phone or computer usage, but a bill from American Express could include everything from meals and entertainment to the purchase of a new computer. Look to the categories on your income statement to find out how the money was spent. (See sidebar "Typical Business Expense Categories.")

The "numbers" generated by the basic reports are, for the most part, common sense and simple math. You don't need an MBA and you don't have to be rigidly systematic about tracking them, but discipline is key. You must make the time on a regular basis to review where you stand and to reflect on the health of your business. Then use that information to grow.

With all this data at your fingertips, you'll be able to anticipate and prepare for a cash crunch. Without it, you may be caught unawares.

## METRICS TO TRACK

With all the basics in place, you can step back and take a broader view of your creative business. How profitable were you last year? That isn't necessarily how much money you made, although you do need to know that. As discussed in the previous section, profitability involves much more than gross income.

How much of your time did you bill for? Did you earn more or less than the year before? Did your work come mostly from new clients or existing ones? Did it come predominantly from one industry or from all over the place? Did it come from one "gorilla client" or a host of smaller clients?

Start by tracking these basic metrics.

## Number of Clients

Do you have enough clients? If you only have a couple big clients but they keep you pretty busy, your plate may be full today, but what would happen if one (or more) disappeared? How would you replace them? Needless to say, it's a precarious position to be in.

The rule of thumb is that no client should make up any more than 20–25 percent of your income. You need at least four or five healthy client relationships, ideally more, so that you are not dependent on any of them.

Diversity in client base is also critical, but it presents another challenge: Should you focus on a target market for efficient marketing, or diversify your income so it's not all coming from the same industry, in case the economy shifts? Again, there's no right answer—only the one that makes the most sense for your business. Don't wait for a crisis to answer it.

## Productivity

Is enough of your total working time billable? Or do you get distracted with administrative tasks (or Facebook)? To know, you must track your time, whether you use a web-based software or do it the old-fashioned way (on paper).

Here's the ideal: 60–75 percent of your time should be billable and 25–40 percent spent on everything else, though often the inverse is the reality. Try reaching for the higher goal and put systems in place to "chunk" your tasks for better efficiency. Also there are online tools to facilitate the process for time-tracking and project management. TimeFox and TimeFox Lite, from FunctionFox, are popular in the design industry because they were created by a designer, Mary-Lynn Bellamy-Willms of Suburbia Advertising. (See Resources section for more online tools.)

## Proposals Converted

Are you doing too many proposals and RFPs that go nowhere? You should be winning one out of every four you do—25 percent. If you're winning more than that, you may not be charging enough. If you're winning less, you may not be qualifying your prospects well enough.

These metrics and more will help you become profitable, which is the ultimate goal. Without the facts, you won't know if you're profitable. But what exactly does it mean to be profitable? Read on to find out.

# UNDERSTANDING PROFITABILITY

## BY CAMERON FOOTE

Everyone understands that a company has to be profitable to stay in business. Nonetheless, sometimes it's tough to make a profit and still be competitive. Other times profitability seems at odds with well-developed content. And still other times there's a desire to go easy on favorite or "poor" clients. In situations like these, remember that every low- or no-profit project increases the pressure to raise prices on others. The fairest thing for your clients, and yourself, is to strive for consistent profitability on everything.

**Internally.** Anyone who believes that the need for a reasonable profit can get in the way of doing top-quality work needs to be reminded of the following: Profits are what allow an individual to live a healthy and productive life and allow firms to pay good salaries, have up-to-date equipment and maintain a comfortable workplace. Few individuals or employees would be willing to sacrifice these things.

Moreover, the less profitable a service business is, the less latitude it will have in whom it works with in the future; conversely, the more profitable it is, the more it will be able to turn down unsavory projects and clients. Also, a profitable business will be able to take an occasional financial hit on a project or account gone bad.

**Externally.** There is no reason not to talk about project or account profitability with clients. Most, after all, are profit-making operations themselves. Even managers in not-for-profits understand that their suppliers need to be profitable. Without profits, a supplier couldn't afford to spend time learning about client needs, or even to work with them. And what client would want to invest in educating a supplier about their industry if lack of profitability caused the supplier to fail? Or who wants to work with a supplier with an incentive to cut corners whenever possible?

## BUSY OR PROFITABLE?

On its face, busyness—high workflow—brings in more income, allows costs to be amortized over a larger base and can be personally rewarding. Then, too, being constantly busy provides an aura of prosperity, and is necessary for growth.

Too often, though, busyness ends up as an objective unto itself. Work is pursued without regard to profitability. Pressure and better creativity are mistakenly equated. The objective of a business is not staying busy; it is staying busy with rewarding and profitable work.

Don't confuse activity with productivity, or confuse time spent with time billed, or project income with project profit. Being very busy can easily camouflage management problems or leave little time to address them.

In addition, remember that success and prosperity in a service business are not size-dependent. Larger clients and projects are not necessarily more profitable. And larger size rarely provides greater production efficiency or dramatically reduces costs (scale economies).

Cameron Foote is editor of the *Creative Business* newsletter (www.creativebusiness.com).

## COMPARING YOUR PERFORMANCE
## TO INDUSTRY STANDARDS

"Without metrics," says Rick Gould, a managing partner of StevensGouldPincus, the New York-based merger and management consulting firm specializing in the communications field, "it's easy to be complacent and tell yourself that the way you are running your business is just fine. Without benchmarks, you won't know what to improve upon and how."

It can be very motivating to know where you stand compared to others, although it's not easy information to come by. The problem is, in the creative services professions, there aren't many industry standards to use. Gould's firm annually conducts a benchmarking survey for the public-relations industry, and those metrics can be used as general guidelines for other creative services professionals since the concept and percentages are very similar.

Some networking groups and conferences facilitate discussions on these sensitive topics (such as breakfast round-table-type discussions at annual events and online groups run by Marketing Mentor), but if you can't find one, you can also create your own. All you need are a few open-minded creative professionals who are willing to share.

For example, if you learn that on average, your colleagues generated more business from new clients than you did, you might be motivated to increase your marketing. Or, if you find out that your competitors are getting paid faster, you might change your payment terms or consider taking payment online.

Here are three key benchmarking parameters to aim for:

- 50 percent of your gross income from creative fees should go to salaries (even if it's only your own)

- 25 percent of your gross income from creative fees should go to operating expenses (what it takes to run your business)

• 25 percent of your gross income from creative fees should go to profits (what's left over and can be used as equity or invested back into the business once your taxes are paid)

These are the three most important benchmarks. "Our advice is always to consistently monitor fixed costs, keeping total operating expenses under 25 percent, no matter what size you are," says Gould. "It is very difficult to change course and cut back quickly during less prosperous times. If you hold to these benchmarking parameters, you will provide the appropriate level of service to your clients, hold your payroll to the correct proportion—and take home considerably more money."

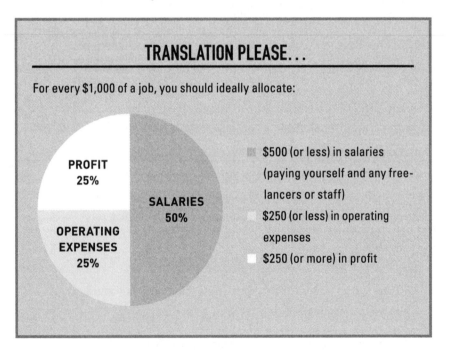

## TRANSLATION PLEASE...

For every $1,000 of a job, you should ideally allocate:

PROFIT
25%

SALARIES
50%

OPERATING
EXPENSES
25%

$500 (or less) in salaries (paying yourself and any freelancers or staff)

$250 (or less) in operating expenses

$250 (or more) in profit

Gould recommends treating your business—and building its value—as if you were planning to sell it, even if you're not. "Looking at your business like a buyer does, you'd be watching your costs, labor, productivity," he says. Even if you have no intention to sell or even retire, a good business person watches the finances closely and stays out of the financial fog. Don't get distracted by client work or by the rest of your life. Look closely at every single number and make changes when they start to move away from the benchmarks. That discipline will hold you in good stead.

# CHAPTER 13
# REQUESTS FOR PROPOSALS

"Creative firms with high win rates do not accept a vague request for proposal and are not in the business of responding to every RFP. Rather, these firms ask deeper questions that help the prospective client specify tangible criteria. Defining criteria enables the client to compare competitive proposals equitably and allows competing firms to customize their responses within the proper context."

**—EMILY COHEN, CONSULTANT TO CREATIVES**

Some creative professionals have a rule: "We never respond to requests for proposals." Often, it's because they have past experience of toiling for hours, submitting blindly and never winning the project.

But rules like these aren't always useful. It's better to have a way to assess each opportunity that comes your way. You need a list of criteria against which you can rate each RFP, and custom proposals too, so you don't waste your time bidding on projects you are unlikely to get.

In an official "request for proposal," an organization, often a large bureaucratic one, puts a project out "to bid" and solicits "proposals" from a few (often too many) vendors, ostensibly in an effort to compare apples to apples. It's the equivalent of a cattle call for creatives.

In some industries, however, all work is chosen through a public bidding system. So if you refuse to take part in the RFP process, you won't do much work in your field.

## TRUE STORY: JULIA REICH ON NOT WINNING THE PROPOSAL

I just learned this morning that I did not win a juicy design and branding project that I submitted a proposal for, in response to an RFP, and am bitterly disappointed. I feel I was an extremely strong candidate—well qualified to handle the work, with a strong creative portfolio.

When I do not win a project, the first thing I do is ask the prospect why. I promptly picked up the phone to discuss the matter with the agency leading the search and was able to learn some things about how the committee made their decision and also how I can improve my proposals for the future.

I learned that the committee—made up of reps from various city and county agencies—used a fair, thorough methodology to score candidates, consisting of categories and a point system. The decision was not based on price. Apparently I came pretty close to the top three firms that made the cut—I came in fourth.

In an ideal world, after I submit a proposal, I should be able to meet with the committee making the decision in order to discuss and answer questions. In this case, unfortunately, insisting on an in-person meeting was just out of the question. Because I was not able to talk to them, they made some assumptions about my work and my proposal that I was not able to defend:

1. The committee questioned my ability to handle the research necessary to complete the branding portion because they thought Julia Reich Design con-

sists of just one person—me—even though I emphasize "my creative team" in the cover letter. Which leads me to wonder if I need to change the name of my company. Does using my name make it sound like I am just one person?

2. The RFP requested copywriting and photography services, and I received low marks here. Why? I do not offer these services in-house so I included names, websites, and ballpark pricing of two highly talented creative free-lancers in the area that I have worked with before, that I would hire as sub-contractors for the project team. Since the scope of work in the RFP for this portion of the project was as-yet undefined, I provided hourly rates for these services and indicated that in some cases, the fees were TBD. How did the firms that made it to the next level include these services? I discovered that they provided a fee range (for instance, $1,200–$1,800) and made it look like these services were provided in-house. The committee may have appreciated the apparent "ease" that comes with hiring a design firm that provides "the whole package." Lesson learned: Next time, I will do the same and save the specifics of each creative team member for the interview stage.

3. Finally, even though I submitted a strong portfolio showcasing several brand identity projects I have done, I found out that the committee chose other firms over mine because of the recognizability of the other projects. In other words, the decision-makers had seen the other firms' work previously in the local community—while much of my client base is in New York City. I am not sure what to do about this. Like McDonald's, is the familiar always preferable? I moved to this small community two and a half years ago from New York City, and I have thrown myself into all sorts of community endeavors and taken on leadership positions in local organizations. In spite of this, are they suspicious of perceived outsiders? Should I take this as a lesson to refocus my efforts back to metro New York?

> Of course, there's no guarantee that the changes I make in my next proposal, based on the lessons I learned from all of this, will win me the next project. But I'm glad I made the effort to call my contact to communicate about the decision rather than fuming silently in my office.
>
> Julia Reich is owner of Julia Reich Design (www.juliareichdesign.com).

The experience of Julia Reich highlights several issues that many creative professionals face. This true story illustrates just a few of the many problems with RFPs:

- The RFP often leaves out essential information without which you can't properly bid.

- Decisions are made by committees often comprised of people who know little to nothing about the work they're commissioning.

- You often don't have a chance to speak to anyone involved in the project, even though most have a Question Process you can take advantage of to get your questions answered.

- You don't have an opportunity to correct any assumptions made, many of which may be incorrect.

## HOW TO DECIDE WHICH REQUESTS TO PURSUE

Rather than relying on any subjective feelings you have about an RFP opportunity, develop a systematic process with specific criteria or a checklist of questions.

The first question should be: What are your chances of winning it? Alan Cutler, author of two books on the subject, *Winning Proposal Writing* and *Understanding the Bid and Proposal Process*, says you should have a 25 percent chance of winning it. One way to determine that is to find out how much competition you have. Ask how many others have been offered the opportunity. If you're one of four or fewer, your odds are good. If they expect twenty submissions, it's a long shot, unless you are the perfect fit. If so, can you make a persuasive argument—in writing and in person if necessary—for why you're the best one for the project, with examples to back it up? Also find out if they give preference to particular characteristics. Some RFPs indicate, for example, "Preference will be given to 'local, minority-owned' etc." If you fit the committee's preferences, you have a better chance of winning.

Beyond that, consider these questions:

1. **Does it align with your goals?** Review the evaluation criteria to see if you meet the committee's requirements. Then read the scope of work to see if it meets your requirements. Is it a good fit? Does it support your positioning? Is the organization one you'd like to work with?

2. **Does it have a healthy budget?** If not, it's probably not worth your time, unless there are other factors that make up for it, such as the opportunity to work with and get to know a group or person on your ideal client list. However, the problem with many RFPs is that they have no budget indicated at all.

3. **Can you speak directly to the decision-makers?** If you can't get through to anyone, think twice before spending your time, which may be much better used reaching out to actual prospects who are a better fit.

4. **Are they local?** You are more likely to win a project from a local company or organization. They may never ask to meet you, but as long as the option is there, it may have meaning to them. If you're not local, you can emphasize your willingness to travel.

5. **How serious is the project?** You may be able to assess this from how well the RFP is written. Poorly written RFPs can indicate that the project owners don't know what they're doing.

6. **Do you have the time?** Will the project fill a spot in your upcoming schedule when you will need work, even if it will take time you don't really have right now? If so, it may be worth doing. Or, if it falls in your lap at a time when you are slow, you may be more available to invest in a complex RFP.

If the project fits these and any other criteria you have but you're still not sure if it's worth your time, see if there's a formal Question Period you can take advantage of to gather more information before you make a decision. This will give you more details about the project as well as some insight into how many competitors you have. You can make your final decision after the questions are answered.

Emily Cohen has worked on RFPs for many creative professionals. Here are some tips from her experience.

## ASK QUESTIONS; DON'T MAKE ASSUMPTIONS

### BY EMILY COHEN

One factor that increases a design firm's win rate is the need to be fearless in asking the right questions. Most design firms simply accept a client's initial request for proposal (RFP) as is, whether it is written or verbal. These firms are afraid to ask deeper questions that uncover the client's true needs and expectations. Making assumptions based solely on instinct or out of fear of "nagging the client" can, and often will, result in a misalignment of expectations, as well as a poorly crafted, generic proposal. In such cases, the price may be based on false expectations.

Often, clients that respond negatively to inquiries for clarification about a project's scope are unqualified clients. For example, they might not be primary decision-makers or they could be less familiar with the value that good design can add to their organization. They may be looking for "order takers" rather than strategic thinkers and collaborators. In such cases, price will almost certainly be the primary criterion in the client's selection process. The larger question is: Do you want a client with so many red flags?

## When There Is No Stated Budget in an RFP

Will a project be worth the time it takes to do the proposal? That's the main question to answer. But often, you will find no mention of budget in an RFP. What to do?

Julie Vail, of Boston-based Marquis Design, was considering a budgetless RFP for a trade association she wanted to work with. She knew the budget wouldn't be big, and she was willing to do it for less than normal. She also had a minimum below which she couldn't go. She decided to do an experiment and ask the question this way:

> 💬 "Since it is stated in the RFP that the primary consideration for selection will be based on price, we'd like to request the opportunity to see if we would fit into your budget range prior to preparing our proposal. As you may imagine, the creation of such proposals is a lengthy process, and if price is of major concern, we would prefer to not waste your time, or ours, if we are not a good fit for each other. We are prepared to give you a rough budget range now based on the deliverables outlined in the RFP, as well as the answers to the above questions. If those numbers fall within your comfort zone, we'd be happy and delighted to put together the full proposal."

In another situation, Sharon Bending of Chicago-based Bending Design pushed a bit with a prospect who wouldn't provide a number by offering one up:

> 💬 "We usually are given a budget range so we can tailor the project to fit within any constraints that may exist. This allows me to gauge whether or not to continue with the RFP process—for example, if your budget for this project is $10,000, I would respectfully decline to participate. That being said, I wholeheartedly understand and respect where you are coming from and will continue with the proposal. I look forward to hearing from you once you've had a chance to review it."

## How to Increase Your Chances of Winning an RFP

**1. Make contact.** Whenever possible, make contact with the prospect to clarify anything you don't understand. In fact, this is a good idea even if you think you understand everything. If you can reach someone with influence, this conversation alone will separate you from those who simply reply to the RFP without any actual contact. And if you do make contact, request a meeting. You never know; they may agree, in which case you'll have a chance to ask your questions and show your work when the competition didn't. That alone will give you a leg up.

**2. Follow the structure of the RFP exactly.** It goes without saying that you should read the RFP carefully, although not everyone does. Beyond that, most RFPs request the response in a very specific order. Don't even think about using your own proposal template. Don't add information they don't ask for. Deliver what the prospect says they need, not what you think they need. (That can come later, if you get the job.)

**3. Get help.** It's best to have two people involved, a writer and an editor, in an RFP you're serious about. Make the investment and hire a professional to either write it for you or, once you've drafted it, have it professionally edited. You can also hire a professional to draft a template for you that you can then tailor to each situation.

## The More You Customize, the More You Can Charge

The experience of Maya Kopytman, partner at New York-based C&G Partners, shows that the more you customize a proposal, the more you can charge—and the more likely you are to win it. In the museum industry, which does almost all its bidding through the RFP process, she consistently prices high and wins big interactive projects. Plus, her proposal documents earn kudos from clients. How does she do it?

"We know that their first impression is based on the proposal," says Kopytman, "so we spend extra time addressing the exact concerns stated in the RFP. By projecting that the actual work will also be as custom and as thoughtful as the proposal, our higher fee is justified."

Doesn't everyone address the exact concerns of the RFP? Although it may seem like a no-brainer, it's apparently not that common. Here's what she means: "We literally take the RFP and highlight in yellow all the bold headlines. We copy and paste those headlines, deleting extraneous words, of course, and this becomes the outline for the RFP. By doing this, we propose exactly what they're asking for. To them, it's magic.

"So if they ask for seven items, we give them seven in the same order. If they ask for bios in item #3, that's where we put them, even if we normally put them in the appendix. It is laborious but easy; you don't have to think. Of course, we sometimes copy and paste from other proposals, but only if it really feels like we are answering this proposal."

The response? "One client said, 'Your price is on the high end but yours is by far the most thorough proposal and appears to be the most custom made to our RFP.' In another case, we were short-listed and the client told us that our quote was the highest, but that they understood the value. Again we heard that our proposal was the least boilerplate and the most relevant to the RFP."

Listen to an interview on when to do an RFP at www.creative freelancerblog.com /money-guide.

# RFP: RECIPE FOR PAIN

## BY DOUG DOLAN

Formal competitive bids don't inspire tender feelings—or good work. Requests for Proposals—one of the more perverse creations of corporate minds—used to be sought out by creative firms as regularly as root canals. But with the recent economic downturn, many have succumbed to necessity. Now more and more of us are preparing 25-page responses to 80-page RFPs outlining all the parameters, considerations and stipulations for, say, a series of simple e-blasts or a tweak to the brand identity.

It's almost breathtaking to see the sheer volume of impenetrable verbiage that goes into these documents—and that we mirror back in our responses, terrified that one procedural misstep will get us rejected. The legalistic language is typically based on the same templates used for contracting snow removal services or new ductwork. Still, we read each opaque clause ten times over to reassure ourselves that we don't really need to indemnify the client to the tune of $5 million for accidents involving faulty equipment.

The last bid I submitted took me twelve hours to write (actually more, but I started feeling so ill I stopped keeping track). When you "win" an RFP, you can reduce your stated fees by about fifty bucks an hour to reflect the time you and your team have spent decoding and responding to it. But that's still preferable to not winning, when those dozens of unbillable person-hours go straight out the window.

Why are so many clients—not just in government, but also in the private sector—hell-bent on issuing these things? Their rationale boils down to three points:

**1. The RFP process is fairer.** Totally untrue, of course. Everyone has their horror stories about supposed "fairness." I was once in a briefing for a six-figure branding project when the client sidled up to me and whispered that the RFP was a ruse: they already knew it was going to the incumbent. So my firm, along with twenty-odd others in the room, didn't have a snowball's chance. Guiltily grateful for the tip, I slipped out during a break.

We've all sat listening to some straight-faced functionary drone on about the fair distribution of projects among firms who've made the preferred supplier list—only to watch all future work go to the same agency that's been doing it for years. But of course we never do more than grumble among ourselves. Because one day the tide of fairness may turn the other way. Who hasn't had a client suggest it would be "a very good idea" (nudge, nudge, wink, wink) to respond to that next RFP?

**2. An RFP yields the best possible value.** No. Indeed, most clients go out of their way to state that price alone will not be the determining factor. Then they write such ornate specs for the "deliverables" that the odds of doing an apples-to-apples comparison are well south of nil. They end up with proviso-laden bids from firms aiming to win the job and then upcharge for every deviation from their deftly worded proposals. And any firm that tries to be honest about what the work really entails only succeeds in talking itself right out of the competition.

**3. A competitive RFP encourages superior-quality work.** Again, no. All bidders, good or bad, are subject to the vagaries of who's sitting across the table. The end client, who's best qualified (one would hope) to judge a bid, is just one voice on a committee of generalists who know zero about the task at hand—especially those visionaries who've devoted their careers to what's known suggestively as "procurement." So there are only two ways a good bid can win: by a fluke or if the person who should really be making the decision is so persuasive that the others collude to have their scores come out right.

What's a better way of doing this? Invite several firms to submit proposals for a project—on their terms. Make price a non-issue by stating what the budget is and asking each firm what it can deliver for that sum. Then assess the bids—they won't be apples to apples, but they will be dollars to dollars—to decide who has the most promising ideas and the best track record. There's simply no need to impose the same absurd constraints on creative work that you would on a tender for repaving the parking lot.

The RFP pendulum will swing back. Private-sector clients, at least, will soon realize that the attempt to impose "objectivity" actually scares away good partners and frustrates frontline staff—who resent the lack of faith in their ability to manage supplier selection, and who end up apologizing to bidders (if not conspiring outright) over an embarrassingly rigid process.

In the meantime, I've joined the growing ranks of creative suppliers who help corporate clients prepare their RFP submissions. In the past year, I've earned more from writing boardroom-to-boardroom bids than from any RFP projects I've bid on myself. The process is still a nightmare—but at least with these proposals, I always win.

Doug Dolan is a Toronto-based writer and communications consultant (www.dougdolan. com). This article originally appeared in *Applied Arts* magazine (www.appliedartsmag.com).

# CHAPTER 14
# NEGOTIATING THE CONTRACT

### *DISCLAIMER: I AM NOT A LAWYER

"We see things in black and white: 'They either want me or they don't. I'll either get it or I won't. They will pay this price or they won't.' But between those two poles, there are many other possibilities, if only you would take the time to talk about them, address them, propose them."

**—MIKELANN VALTERRA, CERTIFIED**
**FINANCIAL RECOVERY COACH AND AUTHOR**

Every business book you read will tell you that you need a contract for every client and every project. But in the real world of doing business, it's easy to let this detail slip through the cracks, especially if you aren't particularly comfortable with it in the first place. Is it because you don't have a good contract? (If you read this chapter, you won't be able to use that excuse anymore.) Or because it's an extra step in the process to get things in writing? Or because the job is a rush and there simply is no time to get a contract signed? (How long does it really take?)

If you've been stiffed or had to absorb a cost you couldn't afford thanks to lack of a contract, you have hopefully learned from the experience. If you haven't been lucky enough to have a bad experience yet, read on...

## WHAT IS A CONTRACT, AND WHY DO I NEED ONE?

You need a contract because human relationships are messy, memories are imperfect and communication is often ambiguous. A contract cannot protect you from any of this, but it can bring some clarity and consensus.

Clarity because it puts in writing what was said (and sometimes not said) so all parties can review it before embarking on a joint project. Consensus because each party must agree to what is written before proceeding further. If any problems arise afterward, the contract stands as the objective document to fall back on.

Simply put, a contract is a document that can protect all parties by avoiding misunderstandings and serving as a paper trail if things do go wrong. It outlines the terms and conditions under which you will perform your work, what you will provide to the client and what they will provide in return. Its purpose is also to anticipate problems and clarify the responsibilities of both parties should problems arise.

A contract isn't necessarily a thick document with lots of legalese. A contract can be a simple outline of the terms and conditions by which you and your client agree to work. Or it can be a complex document of several pages, depending on the intricacy of the project or the number of elements involved. Its purpose is to set forth the terms of work—deadlines, scope of work and limitations, contingencies in case of unexpected changes and potential misunderstandings. More than anything, putting these items in writing prevents miscommunication and keeps everyone's stress level low.

Many creative professionals believe that contracts are only necessary for big jobs with big fees for big clients. They often skip the paperwork on small projects. But it's actually the little stuff that has the most potential to cause time-consuming, expensive problems.

Contracts are especially important for creative professionals because when you sell your work, you essentially are selling a right to your property—in this case, your intellectual property, which is intangible. And because it's intangible, the process may be less clear than if the object in question were tangible, like a car or a house.

However, a contract is only as good as the people signing it. Business relationships are built on trust. In fact, many agreements are made on a handshake and that is enough if both parties are trustworthy. So the rule to live by is this: If you sense that your partner is not negotiating in good faith, walk away. Nothing you put in a contract will protect you.

What about a contract's ability to anticipate what might happen? In real life you can't predict everything that could possibly happen, so don't spend too much time thinking about every single "what if." If you're dealing with honorable people, you'll come up with an acceptable solution to an unanticipated problem, even if it's not in the contract.

That said, have your own contract drawn up by an attorney who understands creative services and your interests. You can customize it for each situation. If that's beyond your means, there are plenty of resources available.

See www.creative freelancerblog.com /money-guide for more contract resources.

## SAMPLE CONTRACT

Gerry Suchy's sample contract is download- able from www.creative freelancerblog.com /money-guide.

Gerry Suchy of Arlington, Virginia-based GMS Designs has generously shared his standard contract, created by his in-house legal team (his wife, who's a lawyer). "Clients love it for its simplicity," says Suchy, "and my wife would be the first to tell you that almost all legal documents are mash ups of documents that preceded them. The law firm rule is don't waste time reinventing the wheel if there is a document that can be cut and pasted."

This contract is obviously created for a small design business, but the concepts and language are general enough that they can be adapted for other creative professions. So feel free to adjust this sample contract for your own purposes.

### 1. CLIENT INFORMATION

Name: _____

Organization: _____

Address: _____

E-mail address: _____

Phone number: _____

### 2. PROJECT INFORMATION

Artwork will be designed to enhance the body copy supplied by the client and laid out for an 8.5 x 11, duplex, full-color, trifold brochure. All artwork will be done to client specifications and use client-provided graphics. GMS Designs may supplement other graphics with the approval of the client. Any custom graphics obtained from image houses will be paid for by the client. The project will be designed using some combination of Adobe Illustrator, Adobe Photoshop and Adobe InDesign. The final artwork will be output in a file format suitable for commercial printing press production. If the client does not have a commercial printer, GMS Designs will make three (3) recommendations.

Go into as much detail as possible about what you will do and how you will provide the deliverable.

### 3. PROJECT PRICE AND PAYMENT TERMS

The project price is based upon a negotiated package price for the entire project of $_____ .

The price quote does not include combined a (state) sales tax of 8.0%. Sales tax will not be applied to non-Virginia residents. Additionally if you choose PayPal as your form of payment, there is a service charge that will be computed based on the total payment. This will be itemized and added to the final invoice.

Be sure to note any details regarding state taxes that apply (or don't apply) as well as any service charges you plan to add if you use any services, such as Paypal or other merchant services that charge a fee. It is up to you whether you pass this fee on to your client or absorb it as a cost of doing business. Either way, it should be stated up front and agreed upon. Being able to offer credit card payment helps because small projects can require a very quick turnaround.

## 4. FINAL PAYMENT TERMS

An itemized invoice will be provided to the client within three (3) days of project completion, before the final work files are given to client. A deposit of 50% is required to commence work. Final payment is required when the work is complete. In addition to PayPal, I also accept corporate or business checks. Checks will need to clear before the final files are sent.

There are no "right" terms. What's important is that you outline your terms clearly. Always include how much you'll be paid and when, plus your policies regarding late charges. Traditionally, clients with whom you've maintained long relationships should pay "net thirty," meaning they have the standard thirty days to pay. For smaller projects and for new clients, it's customary to request 50 percent in advance and the balance on delivery.

For large projects, consider asking for "progress payments" which are payments that are not tied directly to project milestones, but instead are tied to the calendar. For example, for a project that you estimate will take you four months, propose four equal monthly payments (less the deposit) on the first of every month. This way, if the project takes longer or the client has a bottleneck, your cash flow isn't compromised. Plus it's an incentive to finish the project since they've already paid for it.

## 5. REVISIONS

The project price quoted does not include an unlimited number of revisions. I, of course, want you to be satisfied with the final look and feel of the project and I'm sure you feel the same. It has been my experience that good communication between the designer and the client can limit the revisions to just minor changes rather than complete do-overs. Minor changes and adjustments are part of the process. Do-overs are a symptom of poor communication. Having said that, let me suggest that for the proposed cost of this project I will include two rounds of adjustments. Beyond that, the cost of further adjustments can be negotiated. This way of doing business works to your advantage as well as mine in that your project is finished in a timely manner and within your budget.

What's important here is addressing the issue of revisions and clarifying exactly what a revision is. It is not advised to provide unlimited revisions at a fixed price, especially with a new client. (See Chapter 8: Talking Price and Negotiating for more details about revisions.)

### 6. OWNERSHIP OF ARTWORK/FILES

Until full payment has been made, GMS Designs retains ownership of all original artwork/files or parts contained therein, whether preliminary or final. Upon full payment, the client shall obtain ownership of the final artwork/ files to use and distribute as they see fit. GMS Designs retains the right to use the completed project and any preliminary designs for the purpose of design competitions, future publications on design, educational purposes, marketing materials and portfolio. Where applicable, the client will be given any necessary credit for usage of the project elements. Any trade-sensitive information, such as product pricing or customer data, shall be redacted by the designer prior to use.

Whether you retain ownership of the files or you transfer that ownership to your client is your decision to make. It should be decided on a case-by-case basis. Here, Suchy is transferring all rights in exchange for full payment, while retaining the right to use the material for promotional purposes. If you want to retain the rights and the native files, you must make that clear because most clients do not understand that is not what they're contracting for.

## 7. PRODUCTION SCHEDULE/DELIVERY OF PROJECT

The client will assume any shipping or insurance costs related to the project. Any alteration or deviation from the above specifications involving extra costs will be executed only upon approval with the client. The designer shall not incur any liability or penalty for delays in the completion of the project due to actions or negligence of client, unusual transportation delays, unforeseen illness, or external forces beyond the control of the designer. If such event(s) occur, it shall entitle the designer to extend the completion/delivery date, by the time equivalent to the period of such delay.

This clause is designed to avoid the all-too-common situation where a client is delayed in getting their feedback to you and you therefore have less time to implement the changes. It states up front that you will extend your time frame according to the length of their delay. In the actual situation, that may not be possible or your choice, but at least you've provided for it as an option.

## 8. THIRD-PARTY SHIPPING

In the event any material necessary for the production of the project must be shipped to a third party for additional processing, typesetting, photographic work, color separation, press work or binding, the designer will incur no liability for losses incurred in transit, or due to the delay of the shipper of the third party.

## 9. CLAIMS PERIOD

Claims for defects, damages and/or shortages must be made by the client in writing within a period of ten (10) days after delivery of all or any part of the order. Failure to make such claim within the stated period shall constitute irrevocable acceptance and an admission that they fully comply with terms, conditions and specifications.

## 10. PROOFING OF FINAL PROJECT

The designer shall make every effort to ensure the final product is free of any grammatical and spelling errors, before giving the final product to the client. It is agreed that it is the client's responsibility to ensure that there are no spelling or grammatical errors contained in the final product. It is agreed that the designer is not responsible or held liable for any errors contained in the final product after the final product has been committed to print or posted in view of the public.

These clauses attempt to protect you from mistakes and minimize your liability. These mistakes will hopefully not occur often but when they do, it can be catastrophic if you haven't protected yourself.

## 11. CANCELLATION

In the event of cancellation of the project, ownership of all copyrights and the original artwork and disks shall be retained by GMS Designs (Gerry Suchy), and a fee for work completed, based on the contract price and expenses already incurred, shall be paid by the client.

It's a good idea to have a clause outlining what will happen and what charges will be incurred in the event of a cancellation of the project. If the cancellation is due to reasons beyond your control, a kill fee should be applied according to a percentage representing the stage of the work completed. The *Graphic Artists Guild Handbook* states, "Typical charges for services rendered can be 25–50 percent if the work is killed during the initial sketch stage, 50 percent if killed after completion of the sketch stage and 100 percent if killed after the final design is completed." You should also allow for payment in the event that the work is rejected due to client dissatisfaction, which also depends on where in the process the project is. GAG also states, "Common cancellation fees are one-third of the total fee if canceled before completion of final art, and 50–100 percent after the final artwork is completed." This is subject to negotiation but should be provided for.

## 12. CONFIDENTIALITY

All correspondence and documents provided will be treated as confidential between the client and the designer, unless consent has been granted by both parties involved.

## 13. ACCEPTANCE OF AGREEMENT

The above prices, specifications and conditions are hereby accepted. The designer is authorized to execute the project as outlined in this agreement. Payment will be made as proposed above. This agreement is not valid until signed by client and returned to the designer.

Signature: _____

Date: _____

Please print your name here: _____

# BAD CONTRACTS/BAD DEALS AND HOW TO GET OUT OF THEM

### BY JEAN S. PERWIN

In the poem "The Hand That Signed the Paper," Dylan Thomas wrote, "Great is the hand that holds dominion over/Man by a scribbled name." All of our hands have signed papers we wish we didn't. But when it happens in business and someone holds dominion over you, figuring out your options can be difficult indeed. If every business relationship went smoothly, no one would ever need to sign or enforce a contract. One of the reasons to have a written contract is to prevent problems and to solve them. What happens if you sign a contract with a client or partner or employer or employee and you live to regret it? What do you do?

First, you have to identify what makes a contract a bad one. A bad contract usually comes down to one of two things: the deal itself is bad or the contract was badly drafted, or both. If the deal you made turned out to be a bad one, the best-drafted contract cannot turn it into a silk purse. But it should be able to help you change it. If the deal is sound, but the contract is poorly drafted, it won't be able to help you solve problems that may come up. But if the deal is bad and the contract poorly drafted, you're down that river and contemplating your lack of a paddle.

If nothing is permanent but change, a good contract anticipates change. And while it's impossible to anticipate every thing that could possibly go wrong, there are several issues that come up often enough that every "good" contract should deal with them.

**Money.** Money is always a problematic issue in any business relationship. While most agreements specify how much money one party is supposed to be paid by the other, a common problem is how and when. If the contract doesn't say specifically (1) when payments are supposed to be made, (2) what happens if they are not, (3) what has to be done before payments are made or (4) how long after invoices are payments due, there will be problems.

**Ownership.** In the creative services business, any agreement that does not spell out who owns what when will be problematic. Copyright ownership is the coin of the realm for designers. Agreements should be very clear about when and if rights transfer to the client. Also, pay close attention to work-for-hire language. Much to their chagrin, many creative professionals have discovered belatedly that they signed work-for-hire agreements.

**Terms.** How long a contract will last can often be the difference between a good contract and a bad one. I have never had a client who regretted signing too short an agreement. But many rue the day they signed long-term agreements. While it can appear very appealing to sign a five-year contract with a client for a monthly retainer, for example, for a specific type of work, five years is a very long time in any business. What looked like a great deal in year one can be strangling you by year three. Short term agreements—no more than one-year with the opportunity to renew—are much safer.

**Termination.** Every agreement should have a way out. The simpler, the better. "This contract may be terminated with 30 days written notice by either party." A bad contract may spell out the work to be done and how you will get paid… but not what happens if you are not paid or if the client rejects the work. A bad contract includes nothing about ownership of the copyright for the work that is created. It does not address how the agreement will end or specify a term after which the parties would have no obligation to each other. It may contain an attorney's fees provision, but may also include an arbitration provision, which has legal implications you may not understand.

## HOW TO GET OUT OF A BAD CONTRACT

There are essentially two ways to get out of a contract—renegotiate it or break it. There are advantages and disadvantages to both.

To renegotiate a contract, you need the other side to be willing to negotiate. If the relationship is still amicable and there's an avenue to work out a new agreement, take it. Sit down. Explain your position and why you need the agreement amended and what kind of terms you are looking for. Remember that you need the cooperation of the other side, so accusing them of bad behavior, even if it's true, is not helpful.

The advantage of breaking the contract is that you end the relationship— either in writing or orally. The disadvantage is that you may be legally liable for payments or for providing services for which the other side could sue you. From where I sit, litigation is always something to be avoided if possible. It's time consuming, expensive and rarely satisfactory. But unfortunately, sometimes it's unavoidable. If you are considering walking away from a contract, get legal advice to determine whether the cost of walking is worth the potential cost of litigation. Then at least if you decide to take the leap, you're not diving into an empty pool.

The best way to avoid bad contracts is to not get into them in the first place. It is often said that an attorney who represents himself has a fool for a client. I would add that a creative professional who drafts his or her own contracts also has a fool for a client.

Jean S. Perwin is a Miami-based intellectual-property attorney who has expertise in creative services.

## THAT'S IT

It's not all that complicated, right? Hopefully you've learned a few things and feel a little less stressed about it all.

Which is not to say that you're now a financial whiz. That doesn't happen overnight and may never.

But at least you know there's an alternative to the weirdness about money. Keep this reference handy so that when situations come up and you feel that familiar weirdness taking over, you can snap yourself right out of it, reach for the book (or link to www.creativefreelancerblog.com/money-guide) to get a little reality check.

And if you need help, let me know.

# RESOURCES

Here are additional books and websites to explore.

## BOOKS

### by Ilise Benun

*The Designer's Guide to Marketing & Pricing* (co-authored with Peleg Top)
*The Creative Professional's Marketing Plan + Calendar*
*Stop Pushing Me Around: A Workplace Guide
    for the Timid, Shy and Less Assertive*
*The Art of Self Promotion*
*PR for Dummies* (Second Edition, co-authored with
    Eric Yaverbaum and Robert W. Bly)
*Designing Websites:// for Every Audience*
*Self-Promotion Online*

### Other Recommended Books

*Business and Legal Forms for Graphic Designers* by Tad Crawford
    and Eva Doman Bruck (with a CD of business form templates)
*Getting to Yes: Negotiating Agreement Without Giving In* by Roger Fisher
*Graphic Artists Guild Handbook: Pricing and Ethical Guidelines*
    (13th edition)
*Graphic Designer's Guide to Pricing, Estimating & Budgeting*
    by Theo Stephan Williams

*Self-Employed Tax Solutions* by June Walker

*Talent Is Not Enough: Business Secrets for Designers* by Shel Perkins

*The Business of Graphic Design: A Sensible Approach* by Ed Gold

*The Business Side of Creativity* by Cameron Foote

*The Creative Business Guide to Running a Graphic Design Business* by Cameron Foote

*The Money Book for Freelancers, Part-Timers, and the Self-Employed* by Joseph D'Agnese and Denise Kiernan

*Understanding the Bid and Proposal Process* by Alan Cutler

*Value-Based Fees: How to Charge and Get What You're Worth* by Alan Weiss

*Winning Proposal Writing* by Alan Cutler

## WEBSITES AND BLOGS

### www.marketing-mentor.com

Home of Marketing Mentor, the coaching program for creative professionals founded by Ilise Benun. Sign up for a free mentoring session and Quick Tips from Marketing Mentor.

### www.marketing-mentor-toolbox.com

Do-it-yourself tools and resources to grow your creative business.

### www.marketingmixblog.com

The official blog for Marketing Mentor, where you'll find success (and horror) stories from and about creatives running their own businesses.

### www.creativefreelancerblog.com

Business advice and inspiration for the creatively self-employed, companion to the Creative Freelancer Conference (www.creativefreelancerconference.com).

**www.creativebusiness.com**

Cameron Foote's site, chock full of resources, forms, articles and the newsletter *Creative Business*.

**www.downtoearthfinance.com**

Galia Gichon's site, an independent resource dedicated to educating clients about investing and financial control and home of www.my moneykit.com.

**www.emilycohen.com**

The site of Emily Cohen, consultant to creative professionals.

**www.junewalkeronline.com**

June Walker's site, with tax advice for the self-employed. Check out her blog for any tax questions.

**www.savvywomenearning.com**

Mikelann Valterra's blog. (Also see www.ratesettingtoolkit.com.)

**http://cpm.aiga.org**

The AIGA Center for Practice Management, resources to help with the daily management of your studio.

**www.vlany.org/resources/index.php**

Resources from Volunteer Lawyers for the Arts.

**www.mint.com**

An online service to help manage your money.

**www.functionfox.com**

Time-tracking software; mention Marketing Mentor for a discount.

# GLOSSARY

It's another language that surely you, as a creative professional, weren't born to understand. No need to try. Here are some basics you've run across in this book. There is a much more comprehensive glossary on www.mint.com.

**Budget:** a list of all planned expenses and revenues.

**Cash flow:** the movement of money in and out of a business for a given period of time.

**FICO Score:** your credit score used by lenders, which assigns a numerical value to a borrower's credit history. The higher your credit score, the less of a risk you are in the eyes of a lender.

**Fixed expenses:** bills you have to pay every month, no matter what, such as rent, utilities, insurance, etc.

**Gross income:** a person or company's total taxable income—including salary or wages earned, capital gains, interest income, dividends, royalties, rental income, etc.—before any and all deductions or taxes are taken out.

**IRA, Roth:** an investment account into which you make after-tax contributions that can therefore be withdrawn tax free.

**IRA, SEP:** an investment account designed for the self-employed, with higher contribution limits than a traditional IRA. It is also tax deductible and tax-deferred, meaning you pay taxes when you make withdrawals.

**IRA, traditional:** an investment account that allows you to save each year a certain amount (cap is set by the IRS) towards your retirement; contributions are tax deductible.

**Net income:** a person or company's total income after taxes and other expenses and liabilities have been deducted—essentially the profit. If expenses exceed income, there is a net loss.

**Variable expenses:** bills you have the option to pay and/or can reduce when necessary.

# PERMISSIONS

"RFP: Recipe for Pain" by Doug Dolan © 2010, reprinted with permission from Doug Dolan and originally published in *Applied Arts* magazine, 2010.

"No Surprises" by Cameron Foote, © 2010, reprinted with permission from Cameron Foote and originally published in *Creative Business* newsletter.

"Understanding Profitability" by Cameron Foote, © 2010, reprinted with permission from Cameron Foote and originally published in *Creative Business* newsletter.

"The Reality of Client Budgets" by Cameron Foote, © 2010, reprinted with permission from Cameron Foote and originally published in *Creative Business* newsletter.

"What is a Price?" by Cameron Foote, © 2010, reprinted with permission from Cameron Foote and originally published in *Creative Business* newsletter.

"Bad Contracts/Bad Deals and How to Get Out of Them" by Jean Perwin © 2010, reprinted with permission from Jean Perwin.

"How to Find Out the Going Rate" by Mikelann Valterra © 2010, reprinted with permission from Mikelann Valterra and originally published in "How to Set and Raise Your Rates" 2007.

"Seven Ways to Make More Money" by Mikelann Valterra © 2010, reprinted with permission from Mikelann Valterra and originally published in "How to Set and Raise Your Rates" 2007.

# INDEX

time-based, 55–56, 58, 61–62.
    *See also* pricing, hourly
value-based, 46–47, 84
productivity, 186
products, creating and selling, 67
professional colleagues, and market
    research, 54–55
professional development, 162
professionalism
    and delinquent clients, 148–149
    demonstrating, 70–71, 135–136
    profit and loss, 181–183
profitability, 62, 174, 187–188
projects
    declining, 100–101
    final, proofing of, 213
    management of, 186
    timing of, 75–76
    value of, 45
    web-related, 56
proposals, 71
    presentation of, 106–107
    proposals converted, 186
    samples of, 84
    submitting, 83–87
    template for, 84
prospects. *See also* clients
    finding, 90–96
    initial contact with, 106
    new prospect questionnaire, 74
    and process, 80–82
    qualifying, 90–91, 97–101
quality, communicating, 70–71
questions, asking, 72–80, 129–131, 192, 198
QuickBooks, 160, 180–181
Quicken, 160, 180–181
rates. *See also* prices; pricing
    lowering, 63, 66–67
    raising, 53, 63–64, 67
    researching, 53–55

records
    financial, 62
    record keeping, basic, 177–179
    monthly, 175
red flags, 98–99
references, 71
referral fees, 67
referrals, 74
Reich, Julia, 193–195
Requests for Proposals, 73, 84, 192–204
    contact regarding, 199–200
reserves, cash, 158
resources, 220–222
retainer arrangements, 57–60
retirement plans, 168–169, 222–223
return on investment, 12–13, 118
revisions
    in contracts, 210–211
    and pricing, 50, 57
    process of, 120–121
Rienzo, Deidre, 36
Rittner, Jennifer, 38
Roberts, Kirk, 26
Roth IRA accounts, 169, 223
S and C corporations, 169
sales, closing, 107, 128–141
savings
    for retirement, 168–169
    short-term, 167
    for taxes, 167–168
scope creep, anticipating,
    120–121, 126
scope of work, defining, 82–83
selection criteria, 76–77
self-assessments
    on managing money, 153
    about money, 9
    on talking about money, 89
self-confidence. *See* confidence
*Self-Employed Tax Solutions*, 163, 177

# TRY A FREE MENTORING SESSION

If you are serious about your business and like the idea of working with a mentor, sign up for a free mentoring session with Ilise Benun.

For more than 20 years, Ilise has worked closely with creative professionals—both solopreneurs and small firm owners—to grow their businesses, dealing with issues from pricing and marketing to business management. Her strength is helping creatives turn their best ideas into action, and she has helped freelancers become small-firm owners and moonlighters make the leap to full-time self-employment.

This really is a free mentoring session—not a sales pitch. During the half hour phone (or video Skype) session, Ilise will answer any questions you have about your business—money, marketing, client relations, time management, whatever's on your mind—she will give you every idea and resource she can think of. And then, if you want to know more about how Marketing Mentor can help you move forward, she'll tell you.

Sign up here: www.marketing-mentor.com/html/contact.html (and also listen to a sample free session), or fill out the form on the next page and fax it back to: 866-954-5810.

## I'D LIKE TO GET MORE INFORMATION ABOUT MARKETING MENTOR...

| | |
|---|---|
| Name:<br>Company name:<br>E-mail address:<br>Phone:<br>Location and Time Zone: | I am a:<br>☐ Solopreneur<br>☐ Small-firm owner |

| I've been in business: | I need help with (check all that apply): |
|---|---|
| ☐ Less than 1 year<br>☐ 1–5 years<br>☐ 5–10 years<br>☐ More than 10 years | ☐ Marketing<br>☐ Money<br>☐ Time management<br>☐ Client relations<br>☐ Other |

Are there specific issues you'd like to discuss? If so, write them here:

# CHECK OUT ANOTHER GREAT BOOK
# FROM MARKETING MENTOR

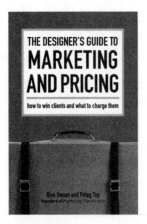

**The Designer's Guide to Marketing and Pricing**

*The Designer's Guide to Marketing and Pricing* answers all of the common questions asked by creatives every day. This nuts and bolts guide to running a creative services business teaches you how to create a smart marketing plan—along with small actionable steps to take to reach your financial goals. From learning which marketing tools are most effective and how to use them to discovering how to establish contact with potential clients, this book is the must-have guide for navigating the murky waters of the design business.

#Z1042, 288 pages, paperback, ISBN: 978-1-60061-008-0

**Find this book and many others at www.MyDesignShop.com or your local bookstore.**